ANGER AND FORGIVENESS

Anger and Forgiveness

How Can You Win the Battle?

Mipo E. Dadang

AFRICA CHRISTIAN TEXTBOOKS

2018

Anger and Forgiveness
How Can You Win the Battle?
© 2018 Mipo E. Dadang

Africa Christian Textbooks (ACTS)

ACTS Bookshop, International HQ, TCNN,
PMB 2020, Bukuru, Plateau State, 930008, Nigeria
GSM: +234 (0) 803-589-5328; E-mail: pa@actsnigeria.org
Website: http://actsnigeria.org

ISBN: 9789789053940 Print
ISBN: 9789789053957 ePub
ISBN: 9789789053964 Mobi

DEDICATION

This book is dedicated to Dr. Samuel Ogiri, BM, BCH (Jos), MPH (Leeds), Public Health Specialist, my accountability partner whom I had a rare privilege to disciple at ECWA Unity Church, Rayfield, Jos Nigeria. His Christian maturity and commitment to holistic service has propelled him to continue to disciple others as a way of life as he serves as works elder in the local church where he was discipled.

CONTENTS

FOREWORD

Who hasn't been wronged by someone unjustly in their lives? Ever since Cain killed Abel in Genesis 3, the world has been a place where sin has ruled and injustice has been the consequence. So it is natural that the creation would groan under the weight of the sin that man has brought on it (Romans 8:18-21). Even the one who came to set it right, Jesus the Messiah, was crucified by the very ones He came to save.

If there were ever a time that a book such as this was needed, it is now. Violence has become the new "normal" today. An Internet search uncovered fifty-nine armed conflicts going on in the world today, with seven of the top fifteen wars active at the time of this writing being in Africa. Enter African Christians, and one is faced with a dilemma. What should one do when one has been forgiven by God through faith in Jesus Christ, and then suffers at the hand of those who, like Cain, claim the authority to be able to make their own judgments of what is right and what is wrong? Haven't there been times when we, like Peter, felt we had to take justice into our own hands when he used his sword to defend the One being arrested that night (Luke 22:49)?

Dr. Mipo Dadang is just such a man. As a Nigerian believer, he has stood for his faith in Jesus Christ. He speaks deeply from his heart and personal experience as he addresses the theological perspective of a Christian's response to violence. His thoughtful response helps us think through how to suffer for Christ's sake while actively pursuing peace with those who are not followers of Jesus. This is a must-read for Christians who seek to imitate Christ. There is not even a hint of bravado in his writing; only simple humility in reflecting on the believer's reaction to his enemies. The power from his words comes only from holy boldness.

Forgiveness is not child's play. While the modern cliché goes, "I will forgive but never forget," the author focuses our thoughts on the weakness of our own willingness to forgive. He challenges us to show God's grace in the same way and to the same extent that we have received it from God. This is a book the Christian will need to read and re-read.

Professor Marc Wooten, USA

February 2018

PREFACE

I was invited by the ECWA Plateau District Church Council meeting in 1991 to lead a devotion. It was my first time to appear at a council meeting. I was nervous. Because I entertained fear, I made up my mind to sit at the door of the conference hall. However, before the meeting started, my senior pastor, who was a member of the council, arrived. When he saw me, he was very upset and wondered what I was doing in a place where I was not qualified. He asked, "Young man, why you are here? This meeting is not for young people like you. Get up and leave immediately." I picked up my Bible and hurriedly left the venue of the council meeting. I did not know that one of the district church leaders was watching. As I was quick to my feet, he ran after me and brought me back to the meeting. I led the devotion and hurried back to the former Evangel Hospital (now Bingham University Teaching Hospital Jos) where I was working as a chaplain.

My senior pastor's actions created bitterness in my mind. I wondered why he intimidated me by taking advantage of my youthfulness. I was angry with him. After a time, I wondered if forgiving him could remove the incident from my memory. Later, I realized my forgiveness of him did cut the chains of bitterness that bound me to that memory. It was at this point I started pondering the idea of forgiving from the heart. Eventually, I observed that in pastoral circles and in all leadership levels, people asked questions if it were possible to forgive and forget. During significant counselling with members in my church and outside my church, people asked me to write on forgiveness. Despite those appeals, I was reluctant. It was an extraordinary testimony of an educationist that thrilled me. Listening to one of my talks on forgiveness, helped him to forgive a pastor of another denomination against whom he had held a grudge and bitterness for a long period of time.

Anger can be a twin sister to forgiveness. I came to understand that anger can make someone do foolish things. In pastoral service, I came across people plagued by anger. I watched their impatience, frustrations, and irritation with their children when they were in church. It left members' relationships with fellow brothers and sisters of the same membership in jeopardy. These challenges motivated me to start writing this book. The second part of the book is also practical and biblical. It includes a guide to overcoming anger and impatience whether in church or society.

ACKNOWLEDGEMENTS

I am grateful to God and all those whose life situations shaped my biblical-theological understanding that human beings, no matter their godliness, are limited because of their Adamic nature; they do not have divine power in restraining their moral behaviours.

I thank God that this understanding gave me possible insight to apply the principles of forgiving from the heart.

I also thank all my friends and instructors for helping me write this book out of a biblical perspective and from practical experience.

I thank Binda Zogore and Janet Joseph who served faithfully as administrative secretaries when I was General Secretary of ECWA from 2005-2011. I am grateful to them, and to others, for allowing me to use them as illustrations in the book.

I am grateful to Lovina Donatus for the time she spent in typing manuscripts.

I am grateful to Professor Marc Wooten for the time he spent in editing and revising the manuscript to conform to current requirements of citation and reference.

INTRODUCTION

Forgiveness is a hard subject to write, to teach, to preach, and to live out. This is why some people deny its existence. Other people do not want to think about it. If you are a person who does not easily forgive others, please recognize that writing is not a sign of being an expert as much as it is the result of reflecting on my experiences of forgiving and forgetting what others have done to me. I write from simple and common knowledge. Give this book a trial. The best learning occurs when the writer and a reader share in the experiences of a person who has lived his life forgiving from his heart those who have hurt him in life.

Someone may ask why a book on forgiveness is necessary. It is an attempt to discover the nexus of Christian forgiveness from Scripture. Discovering it leads to an inner healing of the mind, soul, and body as a person, which will have a positive impact on both church and society. As a Christian leader who often works with people plagued by the difficulty of forgiving others, I learned they suffer hot flashes of bitterness that seem to result in an unforgiving spirit. These feelings usually arise from particular hurts those people have experienced in their lives. This bitterness graduates to a stage of not wanting to forgive. As a result, they conclude that those who have hurt them cannot and should not be forgiven. Some of these bitter people claim to be Christians and some are non-Christians. Those who are Christians attend Sunday services regularly. They offer a friendly greeting with a big smile when you meet them in church. They usually appear innocent when you meet them at weddings and funerals. You will meet others on occasions such as installations of newly elected or appointed public and church leaders. They turn on their social face, but deep inside them, they are full of bitterness and an unforgiving spirit. They live their lives in anguish because they have not been released from the guilt of an unforgiving spirit. They find it very difficult to comprehend the teaching and biblical message of practicing forgiveness. They become depressed and ineffective in their Christian faith. They no longer believe in God's power that allows one to forgive and forget. An unforgiving spirit leads to an increase in conflicts in society.

At times, it can escalate to an ethnic or religious crisis. When relationships break down to this extent, it can be difficult to bring about reconciliation and restoration. Forgiveness will help the reader to understand why it is one of the best tools in achieving restoration from the hurts caused by people. This book presents a practical approach in dealing with those whom you may hurt and or those who have hurt you. It is a manual that, when applied, can restore fractured relationships. Unfortunately, forgiveness is rarely discussed or applied in the African Church. Although it is a hard subject to preach, teach, and write about, the burden to explore forgiveness comes out from years of stewardship. Meyer writes:

> If you are alive, you have experienced the need to forgive. Having friends opens you to hurt; being married opens you to hurt; pastoring a church opens you to hurt, being in a leadership position opens you to hurts; being part of a family opens them to hurt and playing on a football team opens you to hurt.[1]

How can this be illustrated in human living?

The need for forgiveness may be illustrated with a simple story of Tonga and Tina. Tonga and Tina got married years ago. One day, Tonga came home from work after drinking *goskolo* (it is a type of

---

[1]Paul J. Meyer, *Forgiveness ... the Ultimate Miracle*, (Orlando: Bridge Logos, 2006), 28.

locally made alcohol). He reacted to a small comment from Tina by raising his voice and shouted at her,

> You don't even care how hard, frustrating, and difficult my day has been! All you do is talk about what you did with your foolish friend.

Having accused his wife, ("you did not care and all you do ...") and being angry, he retreated to the bedroom, slammed the door, and spent the evening in front of the television. Tina was deeply offended by Tonga's outburst and false accusations. Tight-lipped, she also banged the pots in the kitchen in a far-from-silent non-verbal expression of anger. She waited for Tonga to apologize and ask for forgiveness. However, as a very typical African husband, he never did. Worst of all, Tonga and Tina forgot that they were not to "let the sun go down over their anger or get rid of all bitterness by seeking to forgive each other" (Ephesians 4:29-32). By bedtime, however, the volcanic heat of their hot tempers had cooled down.

Indeed, the temperature in the room had plunged far below zero degrees. The bed was like an arctic ice block. There seemed to be an invisible wall of impenetrable ice bricks that divided the bed into half. What were Tonga and Tina expected to do? Should they have just slept over it and hoped things would be forgotten the next morning? Should they have said, "I am sorry and ask for forgiveness," or should they have hugged and kissed each other contrary to the African tradition? What should they have done earlier, immediately that evening when Tonga got angry? This could happen to anyone. While Tonga and Tina are imaginary people, unfortunately, their situation is not fictional. It is lived out a million times a day. It is not just husbands and wives who act out these negative interpersonal relationships.

Tonga and Tina could have been Binda Zogore and Janet Joseph who are co-workers sharing the same office at Noad Avenue in

Jos.[2] They could have been Gloria and Zipporah, church members who attend the same ECWA church youth fellowship. They could have been anyone. Shattered and fractured relationships lead to ugly friendships for all of us. Sometimes, we are the offenders and sometimes, we are the offended. Going our own way affects our relationships with other people. It causes hurts, pains, anger, bitterness, hostility, division and untold misery. That is just on the human level.

More importantly, fractured relationships are not the same as forgiving people from the heart who have offended us. Paul addresses the believers in Ephesus, "not to grieve the Holy Spirit by whom they were sealed for the day of redemption." His admonition to his readers requires that we too do not ignore the importance of the warning he gave. We can bring sorrow to the Holy Spirit by the way we live. He speaks against unwholesome language, bitterness, improper use of anger, harsh words, slander, and bad attitudes towards others. Instead of acting in negative ways, we should be forgiving people just as God has forgiven us. (Ephesians 4:28-32). Every person needs to know it is true that forgiveness is a basic survival tool for living a peaceful relationship. Knowing how to forgive and how to be forgiven is an indispensable component of a godly living.

In the introductory illustration, I suggested that Tonga should not have spoken angrily to Tina. In the same vein, Tina should not have let her resentment against Tonga's action control her. What should they have done? What should you do when you offend someone or when you are offended? Forgiving one another is an important quality that needs to be constantly applied. We are in a world populated by

---

[2]Mr. Binda Zogore and Janet Joseph are faithful secretaries who serve in the headquarters of a Christian organization in Jos, Nigeria. I thank them for allowing me to use them as illustration to draw the message closer home.

imperfect people and in churches populated by saved-sinners. We often handle the need to forgive poorly or not at all. But what is forgiveness in the first place? How do we understand forgiveness in a biblical context that helps human beings develop cordial relationships among themselves?

CHAPTER 1

CALLED TO BE FORGIVERS

It is not possible to start with defining the term forgiveness without discussing issues that concern Christian living. For a Christian, forgiveness among God's people is a normal way of life. Children of God who regularly confess sins and forgive others demonstrate strong faith in Christ, thereby modelling Christian life for the church. This book is designed to help equip people generally in their vocations through the constant practice of forgiveness. God uses different people to lead others–pastors, teachers, elders, organizations, officers, parents, youth, government officials and many others who may not be officially appointed but serve as examples for others. In the constant interaction among people there are many opportunities for hurts to arise and thus the need to practice forgiveness.. Although some people may feel that this subject is rather basic to faith, however, for most people forgiveness is rarely easy nor routinely practiced in life's daily struggles. Nonetheless, when applied consistently in the life of Christians, this one fundamental of the sanctified life makes a profound difference in influencing believers and non-believers.

Every Christian is called by God to serve as an instrument of forgiving others. Sinners who begin to grasp the seriousness of their plight treasure that God has forgiven us while we were yet sinners

(Romans 5:8). Who is more qualified to tell others about this great gift and of the need for forgiveness than those who need it most? Thus God chose us, forgiven sinners, to serve as His representatives in delivering this lifesaving message about the need to forgive others.

Theological Meaning of Forgiveness.

Theologically, one cannot consider the forgiveness of another person outside the context of God's forgiveness. Soares-Prabhu writes:

> The reason the Christian scriptures constantly relate our forgiveness to God's forgiveness is because readiness to forgive others is not just a happy trait of character or an acquired psychological disposition.[1]

Forgiveness involves a religious attitude rooted in the Christian experience of God's love in him or her. God always plays the leading role in forgiveness.[2] Sin is a physical evil for the victim and a moral evil for the perpetrator.[3] The message of forgiveness is that a radical healing of the sinner takes place when they are forgiven. No other mechanism has this power of love than forgiveness. Forgiving with love is the vehicle of hope that love will transform the sinner.

Dumortier writes,

> Forgiving is the ability to envision a future which would not be built on the past and at the same time; the past exists as part of one's life.[4]

---

[1] G. Soares-Prabhu, "'As We Forgive:' Inter-Human Forgiveness in the Teaching of Jesus," *Concilium*, 184 (April), 57-68, 1986.

[2] M. Rubio, "The Christian Virtue of Forgiveness," *Concilium*, 184 (April), 80-94, 1986.

[3] J. Sobrino, "Latin America: Place of Sin and Forgiveness," *Concilium*, 184 (April, 45-56), 1986.

[4] F. X. Dumortier, (1993) "Dimensions Socio-Politiques du mal et du pardon," in L-M Chauvet & P De Clerck (ed.), *Le Sacrement du pardon: Entre hier et demain* (125-138) Paris: Editions Desclee.

This person sees that the strength of the present and the strength of forgiveness opens one to the promise of the future through the God of mercy and God of forgiveness. A person may wonder if forgiveness, understood as revealed and incarnated in Jesus Christ, is impossible on the human plane. Forgiveness, as understood in the gospels, shows that humans enter into a new dimension of human relations of God's graciousness and the unselfish love of Christ.

Thus, Patton writes of forgiveness from a pastoral understanding and addresses the question whether human forgiveness is possible? He defines forgiveness not as doing something, but discovering something—that I am more like those who have hurt me, than different from them. I am able to forgive when I discover that I am in no position to forgive. Although the experience of God's forgiveness may involve confession of and the sense of being forgiven for specific sins, at its heart, it is the recognition of my inception into the community of sinners, among those affirmed by God as his children.[5]

Therefore, Patton writes

> Forgiveness is something that one discovers. This view of forgiveness as a discovery is different from the traditional theological meaning of forgiveness as an act, or an attitude, or psychologically behavioral technique of reducing pain is self-injury.[6]

Forgiveness in Religious Views

Let us contrast the teaching on the subject of forgiveness in Christianity with that of certain world religions and traditions. The examples chosen are Judaism, Islam, Buddhism, Hinduism. In the

---

[5]John Patton. *Is Human Forgiveness Possible? A Pastoral Care Perspective*, (Nashville: Abindon Press, 1985), 16.
[6]Patton, 185.

Christian faith, the parable of the prodigal son is a well-known paradigm for the practice of forgiveness.[7] In Christianity, according to Williams,

> Forgiveness is generally understood as an act of pardon or release from an injury, offense, or debt and the forgiver shows compassion, while the forgiven shows repentance.[8]

Yet, some religious doctrinal philosophies place much emphasis on their human shortcomings so find it difficult to forgive. Others make little or no distinction between human and or divine forgiveness.

Hence, McCullough, Pargament, and Thoresen quote Dorff that in Judaism, "mehillah denotes the wiping away of a transgression, that is, forgiveness; while selihah denotes reconciliation."[9]

In Islam, according to Ali, "Forgiveness means closing an account of offense against God or any of His creation, and it must meet the criteria of sincerity."[10]

According to Hallisey "There is no unified foundation against which a single 'Buddhist' concept of forgiveness might be sought."[11] Generally speaking, though, the notion of forgiveness comprises two factors:

---

[7]See the *Parable of the Prodigal Son in Christianity and Buddhism*, 2006. Also, read *Forgiveness: A Philosophical Exploration* (Cambridge University Press, 2007), by Charles Griswold, ISBN 978-0-521-70351-2.; David Hein, "Regrets Only: A Theology of Remorse." *The Anglican* 33, no. 4 (October 2004), 5-6; David Hein, "Austine Farrer on Justification and Sanctification: from Religious Duty to Sanctification," *The Anglican Digest* 49. 1 (2007), 51-54.

[8]Michael E. McCullough, Pargament, K.I., & Thoresen, C.E. *Forgiveness: Theory, Research, and Practice* (New York: Guilford Press, 2000), 20.

[9]McCullough, 20.

[10]McCullough, 21.

[11]McCullough, 21

> First, the removal of an expectation of retribution; and second, the renouncing of anger or resentment toward someone who has offended you. Both factors represent changes of attitude, and both are highly valued in Buddhist cultures, but they are generally kept distinct as quite different virtues.[12]

In Hinduism, according to Temoshok and Chandra,

> Forgiveness has been defined as the unaffected condition of the mind of a person, even while being reviled or chastised . . . also described as absence of agitation of the mind even though there is cause for agitation.[13]

Forgiveness in Christianity

In Christianity, most Protestant denominations teach that a believer receives forgiveness directly through personal and sincere confession of sins to God. The believer completes this by an act of forgiving others once they show a repentant attitude. However, in view of the absence of confidentiality among congregations, many Protestant churches emphasize private confession rather than public confession. By contrast, Catholic and Orthodox churches seem to build on a wrong interpretation of the verse "Whoever's sins you retain, they have been retained" (John 20:23). Some also teach that the atonement Jesus offers on the cross is the vehicle through which God forgives the believer of his or her sins. Conflict in a world tainted by sin is inevitable. Every day we breathe, we wrestle with two natures: the sinful nature inherited from Adam and the new creation founded in Christ. In confession and forgiveness, Christians live the Good News and share the Gospel with others. Confessing sin is a profession of our faith in Christ, giving witness to our confidence in God's forgiveness. Forgiving the

---

[12]McCullough 22.

[13]McCullough, chapter 3, 48.

sins of others is the purpose for which Jesus sent us into the world. Forgiveness is the daily exercise of faith for Christ's followers.

Confessing sin is a profession of our faith in Christ, giving witness to our confidence in God's forgiveness. Forgiving the sins of others is the purpose for which Jesus sent us into the world. We frequently miss them because we are too accustomed to recognizing them or practicing the exercises of forgiveness. When two people find themselves enmeshed in conflict, invariably they sin against one another.

Summary

From a theological view, interpersonal forgiveness is letting go of the negative feelings the perpetrator has caused. Interpersonal forgiveness involves both behavioural and cognitive systems. It is letting go of negative feelings. The choice is not to retaliate, but to respond in a loving way and giving up the right to hurt back. The negative thoughts regarding the offender are changed when the decision to forgive is made. The good and bad aspects of the offender are integrated.

Theologically, forgiveness cannot be understood outside of the context of God's forgiveness without reference to sin and evil. Forgiving the offender is understood from a practical pastoral perspective as something that results in healing. This understanding of forgiveness does not simply reduce it to something to be achieved or a behavioural technique to reduce pain.

Forgiveness is a biblical command. In Christianity, forgiveness is primarily discussed within the context of God forgiving man rather than as human effort. Randall Cecrle argues that both forgiveness and repentance focus on the satisfaction of justice. It means for people to forgive others, they should know God's forgiveness of mankind through the atoning death of Jesus. The Apostle Paul says we are to "forgive as the Lord forgave you" (Colossians 3:13). Paul was giving clear instructions on how to forgive.

> Forgive as God forgave you means to forgive in the same way, using the same means of God's grace used to forgive you and me. And how has God forgiven you and me? He forgave us through the blood of Jesus as the atoning satisfaction of His justice.[14]

In our society, there are times when disagreements, resentments, and conflicts can cause bitterness and set apart people for years without forgiving each other. How does one help the average person or church member understand the importance of forgiveness? How can people really understand how to forgive and forget?

Discussion Questions

1. How are biblical ideas about forgiveness similar in context to traditional ones? How are they different?
2. What do you find the hardest aspect about forgiving someone?
3. What has helped you the most to forgive others?
4. What traditions do you have that help you to repent and forgive others?
5. What factors tend to hinder you from repenting and forgiving?
6. How should a church deal with members when they offend each other?

---

[14]See Randall J. Cecrle, *Balancing the Scales of Justices with Forgiveness and Repentance*, 2007 ISBN 1-6026-6041-7; Collin Tipping, *Radical Forgiveness; Making Room for the Miracle*, 1997, ISBN 0-9704814-1-1; Jeanne Safer, *Forgiving and Not Forgetting: Why Sometimes it's Better not to Forgive*, 2000, ISBN 0-380-79471-3.

CHAPTER 2

UNDERSTANDING GOD'S FORGIVENESS AS THE BASIC QUESTION

What is God's plan in dealing with and reconciling a shattered relationship? Forgiveness is not a superficial action, but God's initiative. In Exodus, God spoke to Moses that He is "slow to anger, abounding in love, faithfulness and forgiving wickedness, rebellion and sin," (Exodus 34:6-7). Oliver writes, "One most important thing about God is He forgives sins."[1] Meyer writes, "God wants us to real and honest."[2] Paul explains to the believers in Ephesus,

> Let all bitterness, wrath, anger, clamor, and slander, and all malice be put away. Be kind to one another tender-hearted, forgiving each other just as God in Christ has forgiven you.
> —Ephesians 4:31,32

This is a demonstration of Christ's law of forgiveness as taught in the Gospels (Matthew 6:14-15; 18:35; Mark 11:35). How are shattered

---

[1]J. P. Oliver and J. "Salach" *New International Dictionary of Old Testament Theology and Exegesis* (5 Vols) Van Gemeren, Willem. A. (ed) (Grand Rapids, Michigan: Zondervan, 1997), 260.

[2]Meyer, 59.

relationships restored? It is through forgiveness. How are we to forgive? We are to forgive just as God forgives. When we offend each other, we are to seek forgiveness. God does not forgive others, but mainly for His mercy. When we understand His mercy, we will want to imitate Him (Ephesians 5:1). If you are a victim of bitterness, wrath, anger or any other offenses, there is a biblical model that obligates you "to forgive just as God in Christ has forgiven you" (Matthew 18:21, 22).

Putting it simply, our forgiveness and God's forgiveness should be the same. Forgiveness is all about how broken relationships are restored. The kind of forgiveness that counts is imitating God's forgiveness. It should help readers to reshape all their thinking about relationships that are shattered and apply God's model of forgiveness that leads to healing. It is not a surprise that Gary Inrig writes, "Where there is the forgiveness of sin, there is life and blessedness."[3]

In the opening story of this book, if Tonga and Tina were to set things resolved between them and forgive each other, they would have been good examples of how God forgives. This principle of God's forgiveness applies to everyone in our society. The question is what is God's forgiveness?

What is God's Idea of Forgiveness?

Why is it necessary to discuss God's forgiveness?

When I started studying the Scriptures after conversion, I came to the conclusion that God's act of forgiveness flows out of His unconditional nature of love towards sinners. The Psalmist dramatically captures God's forgiving nature in Psalm 103 by opening

---

[3]Gary Inrig, *Forgiveness*, (Michigan: Discovery House Publishers, 2005), 48.

and closing with, "Bless the Lord O, my soul."[4] The first reason the Psalmist gives for such an exuberant outburst of praise is explained in verse 3. God is the one who "pardons all his iniquities." In order to strengthen his case in praising God, he draws the reader's mind to the history of God's forgiveness. There is no doubt that this is a reflection on God's mercy and forgiveness on Israel following the golden calf incident in Exodus, through which "He made His ways known to Israel. God is compassionate, gracious; slow to anger and abounding in lovingkindness."[5] The mercifulness of God's character or nature has far-reaching implications on repentant sinners.

The Psalmist confirms

> God has not dealt with His people according to their sins. Nor rewards them according to their sins ... for as far as the East is from the West, so has God removed their transgressions from them.

It is a scientific reality that the East and West can never meet. This is a symbolic portrait of God's forgiveness. When He forgives our sins, He takes it away from us and does not even remember it. We need never be perturbed that God will bring our past sins to remembrance. Rather He forgives and forgets. The human tendency tends to dredge up the ugly past, but God has wiped our record clean. If human beings are to follow God, we need to copy the model of biblical forgiveness that comes from Him by forgiving one another. When we forgive each other, we must also forget the sin! Otherwise, we have not truly forgiven.

---

[4]The author's praise focused on God's glorious works. It is easy to complain about life. But the author's lists give us plenty of reasons for which to praise God. He forgives, pardons our iniquities.

[5]The event described in Psalm 103:7-8 (especially verse 8) could be compared to the wording in Exodus 34:6.

The Psalmist confesses that God's forgiveness enabled the remnant to return to their homeland after the Babylonian exile. They were deeply impacted by their forefathers' obstinate rebellion until God's tenacious forgiveness was applied to them. Referring to the Golden Calf incident in Psalm 103, the worship leaders in Nehemiah prayed, affirming, "God's forgiveness is gracious and compassionate."[6]

I came across an interesting model of God's forgiveness in the book of Micah. After Micah prophesied a stinging rebuke for the sins of Israel, he came to realize God's forgiving nature. He could not avoid the amazing grace of God either, and testified,

> Who is a God like you who pardons iniquity and passes over the rebellious act of the remnant of his possession? He does not retain his anger forever because He delights in unchanging love. He has compassion on us and he treats our iniquity with favour. Yes, you will cast all our sins into the depths of the sea.[7]

Oliver writes,

> In the Old Testament, forgiveness comprises of the removal of sin and the restoration of communion between God and humanity. ... It depends solely on God's love, mercy, and compassion towards the sinner ... and on His readiness to initiate the process of reconciliation and atonement. It requires

---

[6]Seeing how God continued to be with his people Israel, shows that his patience is amazing in spite of their repeated fallings, pride, and stubbornness. He is always ready to pardon (Nehemiah 9:17) and His Spirit is always to instruct (9:20). Realizing the extent of God's forgiveness helps God's people to forgive those who fail them even seventy times seven where necessary (Matthew 18:21-22).

[7]The quotation is from Micah 7:18-19, which is a demonstration of the divine fact that God delights to show mercy. He does not forgive grudgingly, but when human beings repent, gladly offers forgiveness to all who come back to Him.

and usually goes hand-in-hand with the confession of sin, repentance, restitution, and renewal.[8]

So how can we explain this fully?

Understanding and Illustrating God's Forgiveness

Let's return to the illustration used in the first chapter. The couple were angry, resentful, bitter, and sulking as a result of unforgiving spirits. Despite knowing he was wrong, the husband blew up, and refused to admit his fault. Because of his pride, he sat in front of the television watching African music. The wife's initial hurt and shock became hardened and buried in silent bitterness. It burned her slowly and puffed up her resentment. Did the couple imitate God's forgiveness? After I preached on forgiveness in my home church, a woman asked me, "If someone offends me, and the person does not know, should I go and tell the person that I was offended?" It is a great question. I told her, "Yes, if you can be sure that the offender will accept his or her fault" (Matthew 18:15).

In order to understand the text in Matthew 18 and the question asked, it helps to understand the context. Jews were not inclined to rebuke their brothers personally because they were afraid of transgressing the principle that Jesus formulated in Matthew 7:1-5 about taking the log out of one's eyes before pointing to another person's log. In our African context, especially among church members in Nigeria, gossips easily create conflicts between people. The woman's question was, therefore, unique because instead of taking the lead in solving conflicts, most people bury the whole idea hoping it would

---

[8]Oliver, *New International Dictionary of Old Testament Theology and Exegesis* (5 Vols), 260.

all be forgotten the next day. They choose not to apply Matthew's principle of resolving conflicts. Worst of all is for a person to remain with an unforgiving spirit.

David the Psalmist warns that to fail to forgive someone can lead to depression, anger, strife, physical lethargy, alienation from others, mental agitation, instability, indecisiveness, spiritual dullness and forgetfulness.[9] Note that bitterness resulting from a lack of forgiveness is likened to an insolent child who does not take correction. The twelfth chapter of Hebrews emphasizes that bitterness is like a noxious weed that springs up and defiles a whole garden. It describes bitterness as like a cancer that eats the soul. Anyone who allows bitterness to control him or her will destroy relationships. Therefore, do not ignore the mood when you are angry. Like a small root that grows into a big tree, bitterness springs up in human hearts and can even overshadow their deepest spiritual relationships with God. Like the venom of a poisonous snake, bitterness comes when we allow disappointments or hurts to develop into resentment or when we nurse grudges over past hurts. Bitterness brings with it jealousy and dissension in people.

Throughout years of working with people, I have adopted three principles regarding forgiveness. First, point out to people that the key to forgiving others is to remember how much God has forgiven them as individuals. Is it difficult for you to forgive someone who has offended you when God has forgiven you so much? Secondly, grasp the concept of God's unconditional love and forgiveness, which helps you love and forgive others as well. A third key function is to always be an agent of peace to people around you.

As I was writing these sentences, I couldn't help laughing. There was a day when one of my daughters and I had a meeting half

---

[9]The reader should endeavor to read Psalms 32, 38, and 51 with understanding and it will become clear.

way down the kitchen. My daughter likes loud background music as she mops around the house or does the dishes. That day I was working in my study for a paper presentation, so I needed a quiet environment in order to concentrate. Her music loudly penetrated the study preventing me from concentrating. So I went out to the sitting room and asked her to lower the volume of the tape down slightly. She happily did so.

When I returned to the study room, I flicked the door to shut behind me. But the breeze through the study windows caught the door and slammed it shut with a very loud bang. As I turned to my desk, I realized that my daughter, not knowing what has happened, might have thought I had slammed the door in anger at the volume of her music. As I stepped back into the sitting room, she was on her way to the study thinking I might have been angry with her. We both laughed after I explained what had happened. That is the way resolving conflicts rapidly works. Both parties are to follow the biblical way of managing conflicts so that it does not result in resentment.

The second step is to treat unforgiveness as neglecting a covenant. John says,

> If we confess our sins to him, he is faithful and just to forgive us our sins to him, he is faithful and just to forgive us our sins and to cleanse us from all wickedness.
>
> —1 John 1:9

God promises to forgive anyone who acknowledges his or her sins before Him. This means forgiveness is a covenant. It is an agreement to erase the offender's sin–debt in light of his or her admitting what has been done is wrong. Hence, there is the need to ask for forgiveness.

It is interesting to note that it is a common phenomenon among Christians to say, "I am sorry" when admitting they have offended someone. This is a worldly emasculation of the biblical concept of forgiveness. Consider for a moment what the sentence "I am sorry" really means. It means, "I feel bad because of what happened." "Forgive me," on the other hand, means something very different. It means, "I owe you a payable debt because of what I did." If I accidentally step on my wife's toes, I say, "I am sorry" to her. However, if I take a stone and hit her toes with it and injure her seriously, is "I am sorry" really what is needed? In the first incident, stepping on her toe was accidental. I expressed my distress over the discomfort I caused my wife by saying "I am sorry." That was adequate because no wrong had taken place. I wished it had never happened. In the second incident, an offense had occurred. I would be seen as angry and malicious in my actions.

Therefore, I would owe God and my wife a payable wrongful debt because of my attitude and actions. The fact that I felt sorry may and or may not mean anything. Judas Iscariot (Matthew 27:1-6) was sorry after he betrayed Jesus, but his sin was not cancelled because he did not ask Jesus to forgive him. The fact that he felt really sorry about the act he committed did not remove the real guilt of what he did. The fact that he wished he had not done it did not erase his sin debt.

However, the process of forgiveness can be a liberating experience. If it is practised proactively, it can be a wonderful experience in life. Forgiveness occurs because we have been given the ability to make choices. We have the choice to forgive or not to forgive and no one can force us to do either. If we want to forgive someone, no one can stop us, no matter how poorly they may act. This ability to forgive is a manifestation of the personal control we have over our lives. It is nice to reflect upon and feel the respect that we have been given to be able to make such profound choices.

The option to forgive also implies that we have discretion as to whether or not we absorb the offense people caused us in the first place. While forgiving may be a difficult choice for many of us, imagine how our lives would have been if we rarely or never used our power of choice to absorb offense. Since we have choices, would it not make sense to limit the number of times we are hurt or offended so that the need to forgive is minimized? The ability to live life without absorbing offense, without apportioning blame, and constantly forgiving are choices leading to peace. This ability to practice proactive forgiveness happens within four dimensions. Luskin mentions four stages that can lead to forgiveness.[10]

In the first stage, a person is filled with self-justified anger. At some point in your life, you may have been hurt and you are mad at the person you feel offended you. You blame the person committing the offense for how you are feeling. It is their action and not your choice to respond because you feel they are the cause of your anger. You have forgotten that you have a choice on how you will react. So you become angry and convinced that it would not be right to forgive the offender. At this stage, there is usually acute and submerged anger.

The second stage towards forgiveness emerges after feeling angry with someone for a while when you realize that the anger does you no good. It may be hurting your emotional balance or your physical health. You wish to repair the damage to the relationship so you take steps to forgive. You begin to analyse the problem from the other person's point of view or you simply decide to let the problem go. In either case, after an extended period of time, you are no longer angry and you have forgiven the person with whom you were angry. This process can be applied to anger by the offended person, the second person, a third party, or to life in general.

The third stage of forgiveness comes after you have seen the results of forgiveness when you choose to let go of your anger quickly. At this stage, the choice is to feel the hurt for a short period of time, and then

---

[10]Frederic Luskin, *Forgive for Good*, (New Jersey: Harper Collins, 2002), 13.

work to either repair the relationship, or let go of seeing the situation as a problem. In either case, you decided to forgive because you have had chosen to practice it and have the benefit in your life. This could emerge as a situation of being cut off by another car on the expressway or in a complex situation like an affair in a marriage. At this stage, you are aware that the length of time you experience the grievance is primarily up to you to decide.

The fourth stage of forgiveness involves the proactive choice to rarely get angry. This means to forgive in advance a specific offense that could trigger being hurt. This stage often emerges at the same time as some or all of the following thoughts; *I do not want to waste my life in the discomfort caused by anger so I will choose to feel differently. I am able to forgive myself, forgive others, and forgive life and not to blame God. I know it hurts when people do not forgive me. I do not want to hurt other people by my anger so I will let it go. Life is filled with incredible beauty and I am missing some if I am experiencing unresolved anger. I forgive myself for getting side-tracked. People do the best they can and if they err, I can best help them by offering understanding.*

The first step in this process is to forgive the specific offense. Everyone, including myself, operates primarily out of self-interest. I must expect that sometimes, I will be annoyed by someone else's expression of their self-interest. If I can understand that this is an ordinary part of life, what is there to be upset about? If I understand that self-interest is the way that I act, how can I but offer forgiveness to everyone, including myself, for behaving that way?

Not everyone will follow these four stages of forgiveness in an identical manner. Some people we love so much that we are usually at the fourth stage with them being open-hearted and ready to forgive. There are others whom we feel have hurt us so deeply that our supply of goodwill for them is almost dry. With these people we find it difficult to get past stage one. What you need to remember is the power of personal choice and the importance of exercising the choice to forgive so that we can bring peace and healing into our relationships and ourselves.

Luskin writes that the Hebrew and Greek for forgive means to pardon. It means to send away, to blot out, to lift up and carry away and to release from legal obligation.[11] I believe the prophet Jeremiah powerfully explains and depicts God's forgiveness when he says:

> . . . in those days and at that time, declares the Lord, the search will be made for the iniquity of Israel but there will be none and for the sins of Judah, but they will not be found, for I have pardon those whom I leave as a remnant.
>
> —Jeremiah 5:20

When God forgives, you can send out a search party armed with radar, infrared scopes, and satellite reconnaissance photos, but they will not be able to find the sin God has removed.

The parable of the unforgiving slave in Matthew 18 also gives us an important illustration on forgiveness. In the parable, the first slave owed the master a debt of trillions of Naira (or any currency readers may care to name). It was a debt impossible to repay. Nevertheless, when the slave begged his patience to allow repayment, the master went a step further. Matthew writes "And the Lord of the slave felt compassion and released him and forgave him the debt" (Matthew 18:27). The master forgave and he released the slave from the legal obligation of that massive debt.

The most graphic image of forgiveness in all the Scriptures is recorded in Colossians,

---

[11]Luskin, 13.

> When you were dead in your transgressions and the
> uncircumcision of your flesh he made alive together with Him,
> having forgiven us all our transgression.
>
> —Colossians 2:13

Paul goes on to speak in verse fourteen saying,

> Having cancelled out the certificate of debt consisting of
> decrees against us, which was hostile to us, and He has taken
> it out on the cross.

Here is the picture Paul was painting to give an illustration of God's forgiveness. God had in His possession a legal document, "a certificate of debt."[12] On that certificate of debt were recorded decrees against every person. The word "decrees" had to do with God's law. God had, as it were, a piece of paper that listed every one of his laws that we had ever broken. What a horrifying thought! That certificate of debt detailed exactly what humans owed God. Anyone of those hostile decrees by itself would have cost human beings their lives and eternal punishment. The Greek word Paul used here could be translated "erased." The certificate recording our legal obligation to God was rubbed out.

In summary, God's forgiveness is the cancellation of an unpayable debt that the guilty or offended owes to God. It is blotting out or the complete removal of the guilt of the offender. If this is how God forgives, is it possible to forgive other people from our heart? A New Testament verse gives a strong command to forgive one another. It says, "Be kind and compassionate to one another; forgiving each other, just as in Christ God forgave you" (Ephesians 4:32). Christians

---

[12]The only other use of this word in the New Testament is in Ephesians 2:15 where it refers to the ordinances of God's law. Σξαλέιφω was used of the process a scribe went through when he made a mistake. He would laboriously rub the still damp ink off the volume or leather scroll on which he was working and start over.

are created in Christ Jesus for good works. People, whose lives are bounded by the Triune God, live and move in the domain of love. We are a people sealed by the Holy Spirit (4:30), beloved children of God who imitate their Father (5:1), and have been brought into the atoning sacrifice of Christ who gave Himself up for them (5:2). We must walk in love. The neighbour can be the victim of self-assertion as a result of anger (4:25, 26). Christians should impart grace (4:29), and be kind and tender-hearted to forgive (4:32). This is the task and challenge in the next chapter.

Discussion Questions

1.   What does it mean to forgive from the Heart?
2.   Naturally speaking, none of us would want to remember past hurts. Is it necessary to do so in order to genuinely forgive?
3.   How is the crisis of forgiveness between you and God, rather than between you and the other person?
4.   Who continues to have pain when there is no forgiveness: the offender or the offended?

CHAPTER 3

FORGIVENESS AS A PRACTICE

Over the years, I have been a Christian I have come to the conclusion that if you love people and get involved with them, you can count on it that they will disappoint, offend, betray, and/or hurt you. This is an unavoidable consequence of relating closely to people. Gradually, you will have to make a choice, to either withdraw from close involvement with them, or learn how to forgive. This is one reason why Jesus and the apostles insisted that forgiveness is a central motif in Christian love. It is an expression of love, and it enables us to go on loving. Forgiveness is one of the most powerful and liberating dimensions of the Christian life, yet it can be confusing. "Be angry but do not sin" (Ephesians 4:26). There is such a thing as righteous anger. Nevertheless, there is the ever-present danger that it may turn into human spite. Let us examine forgiveness as a biblical model for restoring broken relationships.

Forgiveness versus Bitterness

Paul says, "Be kind and compassionate to one another, forgiving each other, just as in Christ, God forgave you" (Ephesians 4:32). This is God's solution to bitterness, which is associated with "rage and anger, brawling and slander" together with every form of malice. Bitterness is prolonged retributive anger towards another person because of an offense committed. Different kinds of offenses may occasion bitterness. Usually, the more intimate the relationship or the more heinous the offense, the more likely it is that you will struggle with bitterness against your offender. One may become bitter without even being offended personally. We can "take up offense" for another person who is close to us and choose to hate people who may never ever have harmed us personally.

According to the Bible, bitterness arises from choosing a particular response to an offense. This explains why two people can experience the same offense, yet one becomes embittered while the other does not. The reason for this is not that the one person was more susceptible to bitterness than the other. Rather, the latter person chose to respond properly to the offense while the former chose to respond wrongly. This fact is painful to accept when you are bitter, but provides the path of liberation, as we shall discuss later.

What is the lie that bitter people believe? According to them, they have the right of retribution, the right to pay people back for their offenses. Deep within the human heart lies the awareness that somebody has to pay. We have a deep-seated conviction that people should pay for hurting others. The Creator, who hates sin because it offends His character and destroys the creatures He loves, has stamped this conviction into our hearts. It is wrong, however, for us to arrogate to ourselves the right to exert revenge because God reserves this right exclusively for himself. This is why Paul says,

> Do not take revenge, my friends, but leave room for God's wrath, for it is written, "It is mine to avenge; I will repay says the Lord."
>
> —Romans 12:19, quoting Deuteronomy 32:35

When we feel outraged over someone's sin against us, we are operating on God's righteousness. Yet, God says there is nothing like righteous anger without sinning in human life. When we choose to pay people back for offenses committed against us, we are usurping God's prerogative. We are playing God, which is even a more serious offense.

How Do We Identify Bitterness?

Since bitterness is prolonged retributive anger, it always betrays itself in thinking and behaviour that is targeted towards paying the person back for his and or her offense. Many people, ignorant of God's prohibition against bitterness, display their intent overtly. They shout their hatred, plot their revenge, and then boast about it to others. The revenge motif is one of the most popular plot lines in literature and movies, precisely because most people think revenge is right. In a way, this overt bitterness is easier to deal with because it is out in the open. If you know you hate someone, then once you know that God wants you to change your attitude; you can cooperate and forgive with compassion from your heart.

Many Christians deny they are bitter because they know God forbids bitterness. When we have hidden bitterness in our hearts, its symptoms become more subtle, but it still manifests itself later in their relationships with those who hurt them.

We will maintain the right to pay back the offender by cultivating certain mental habits. We may replay the offense in our minds repeatedly. This memory becomes a default setting into which we move when our minds are occupied with other matters. You may ruminate over the offense's negative consequences in your life, such as

you spent three years getting out of debt because the manager fired you unjustly! It was horrible not being able to buy for your children the gifts they wanted. You wore clothes until they were threadbare!

Over time, you learn to clutch and fondle such memories as perverted treasures. As a result, you eventually develop an unrealistically negative view of the offender.

By focusing inordinately on his offense, you magnify his bad qualities and gradually lose the ability to recognize his good qualities. I remember a female director at a government company who frustrated two of her most able employees until both of them resigned from the company. They said they were forced to resign because they were from a different ethnic group. However, her dislike of them was not because there was anything wrong with the ethnic group to which they belonged. Rather, she assumed that they wanted to replace her as the leader (a perverted perception), despite the fact that they were from a marginalized group.

Unfortunately, no matter how much effort we expend to hide it, bitterness causes us to express our right to take vengeance. When God opens our eyes to see it, this can be extremely painful. We rejoice when the offender fails or experiences adversity. Why? Because he or she is getting what he or she deserves. Conversely, we cannot rejoice when he or she succeeds or experiences prosperity. Instead, we get angry because he is unfairly getting off the hook. We have an inordinate desire to criticize the offender. When his name comes up in conversation, we feel a strong desire to say something negative. If the talk is already negative, we add to the negative comments in a way that the person is tainted beyond recognition. If the conversation is positive, we bring people back to reality by reminding people of his faults.

We develop a radar-like sense for finding others who are bitter towards the same person. There is a perverted but exquisite delight in commiserating with another like-minded hater over the wickedness of a common offender. I remember listening to a conversation between a woman and her sister who were sitting together on a bus going to Abuja, Nigeria. They began to speak negatively about their stepfather. This subject dominated their conversations. They fed off each other's criticisms, and their conversation was drained and depressing. Both were enslaved by the habit of bitterness, and oblivious to it. Later I drew their attention to the danger bitterness can cause, sometimes even leading to murder.

Some bitter people devote much of their lives to fantasies of revenge. Such fantasies may simply involve giving an offender a good tongue-lashing, but others may lead to a violent attack. This is why Jesus connected hatred to murder. The vast majority of homicides in most cities of Nigeria are simply an outgrowth of bitterness and harmful thoughts nurtured over time. Usually, taking vengeance revolves in a variety of subtle ways. Some blow up over relatively minor issues that give them a "reason" to spew out their anger that has been brewing for months or years.

I know a man who used to be the Managing Director of an organization but lost his job because the company was dying. Since being fired, he has broken off his relationship with one of his key friends who were part of the executive team, probably because he had been removed from office. Yet would the organization have allowed him to continue in office until the company totally collapsed before realizing his inability to manage the affairs of the company? Others choose to give the offender the silent treatment or to engage in massive rebellion, but denying they are angry when asked. Still others become adept at pushing the offender's buttons until they get angry because it provides additional justification to continue to hate him. Some simply sever the relationship without any explanation.

Bitter people are hurting their offenders to pay them back, but tragic irony occurs. By taking vengeance, they hurt themselves far, far more than they hurt their offenders. Delashmutt writes, "Harboring bitterness is like shooting yourself to hit your offender with the recoil of the gun!"[1] Consider the consequences of usurping God's prerogative.

Consequences of Bitterness Include Emotional and Relational Harm

Bitterness can poison your emotional life. There is a connection between bitterness and depression. Many embittered people complain of chronic, unexplained depression. They no longer have the emotional resilience to adverse circumstances that they once had. God evidently designed us to have an emotional reservoir that acts as a buffer to adverse circumstances. A person can fill this emotional reservoir primarily by cultivating gratitude towards God and by practising love towards others. By contrast harbouring bitterness, saps up much energy and places a real drain on our emotional reserves. Bitter people often find themselves easily depressed.[2]

When you become embittered towards another person, you usually think your bitterness negatively affects only that relationship. You think you can tolerate this sin in your life by isolating its destructive effects from those you hate. However, harbouring bitterness greatly impedes your ability to develop and sustain any healthy relationships.

Some people seem to have a floating bitterness. Their bitterness, for example, is rooted in their attitude towards parents who repeatedly humiliated them. They may live a thousand miles away from their

---

[1] Gary Delashmutt, *Loving God's Way: A Fresh Look at the One Another Passages*, 77.

[2] The reader should reason know that I am not suggesting that bitterness is the only cause of depression. There may be many other causes, including chemical imbalance. I refer those who are in a state of chronic depression to seek for the help of professionals to assist them in discovering the cause or causes of their depression.

parents, yet flare up with incredible anger when anyone embarrasses them. This obviously impedes their ability to develop and sustain close friendships because embarrassment is inevitable. At the time of writing, I remembered a very close friend who had parted from me. There didn't seem to be any particular reason for this break, except that I, in a former official capacity had had to replace my friend with someone more experienced. Since then, any gesture of friendship, including visiting my friend after armed robbers had attacked him, has been misinterpreted. I assume that my former friend still has long-term bitterness against me..

Long-term bitterness has a way of poisoning your personality negatively against people. Embittered people tend to become cynical and full of self-pity. Over time, these destructive attitudes can affect the way people speak and carry themselves. Their voices are angry in tone, their faces hostile and their postures aggressive. Most of us have known people whose bearing communicates that they are deeply angry people. Tragically, such people tend to repel others and become more embittered against people for rejecting them.

Most bitter people complain that their offenders have used their power to wrongly hurt or control their lives. In most cases, this is the truth. People in leadership, a domineering parent, or an abusive spouse have all used their position of authority or trust to take advantage of their victims. The tragic irony is that bitterness perpetuates and increases our offender's control over us. The more immersed we become in rehearsing their offense and expressing our revenge, the more we allow them to dominate our lives. This is why bitter people often become like their offenders in certain key ways. We are victimized by their abusive anger but then we become abusive in our own anger. We are victimized by their controlling behaviour, but then we become excessively controlling in our relationships with others. In a mysterious way, bitterness reduces us to the level of the people we hate. In usurping God's role to judge our offenders, we become like the very people we judge when we forget to abide by the biblical model to forgive from our hearts.

The Spiritual Consequences of Bitterness

The most precious privilege of a Christian life is enjoying the relationship with and closeness to a forgiving God who expects His followers to forgive from the heart. While bitterness will not cause God to reject us, it will eventually rob us of the ability to enjoy our relationship with him. John warns:

> Anyone who claims to be in the light but hates his brother is still in the darkness. Whoever loves his brother lives in the light and there is nothing in him to make him stumble. But whoever hates his brother is in the darkness and walks around in the darkness; he does not know where he is going, because the darkness has blinded him.[3]

Bitterness produces spiritual blindness because it is so profoundly hypocritical. Christians are the recipients of incredible forgiveness. We are guilty before a holy God who has just cause to reject us and condemn us forever. Like the man in Jesus' parable, we expect to make others pay their debts to us while we have our own, greater debt forgiven. We insist on the right to take vengeance on our offenders,

---

[3]Does this mean that if you dislike someone you are not a Christian? The verses in I John 2:9-11 are not talking about disliking a disagreeable Christian brother or sister. There will always be people we will not like as much as others. John's words focus on the attitude that causes us to ignore or despise others, to treat them as irritants, competitors, and or enemies. Christian love is not a feeling but a choice. We can choose to be concerned with people's wellbeing and treat them with respect, whether or not we feel affection towards them. If we choose to love others, God will help us express our love.

but we want to enjoy the benefits of being forgiven by God. This double-mindedness is extreme. If we choose to retain our right to hate others, we forfeit the privilege of experiencing God's mercy and goodness. When we sever this crucial linkage between receiving God's forgiveness and extending it to others, we become spiritually paralyzed. Our Christian lives will shrivel away from what they once were when we allowed the wonder of God's mercy with us to spill out to others. Now what barriers are likely to hinder the proactive of the biblical model of forgiveness His word teaches?

Barriers to Forgiveness

There are only two barriers to forgiveness. One is an unwillingness, which is something each of us can change. The other is a misunderstanding of what biblical forgiveness is all about. Forgiveness can be confusing. Misunderstanding of Scripture and cultural misconceptions can distort its meaning. As we sharpen the focus on God's biblical model of forgiveness, note the issues that have been misunderstood by you and which are the issues of unwillingness.[4]

Forgiveness is not:	Forgiveness is:
Dismissing the offender's moral responsibility.	Dismissing the right to pay back and assuming the responsibility to love.
Mainly a feeling.	Mainly a choice based on truth.
Forgetting the offense .	Deciding not to use the offense in retributive ways.
A once-for-all event.	A decision which must often be reaffirmed.

---

[4]David W. Augsburger, *The Freedom of Forgiveness*, (Chicago: Moody Press, 1980), 28.

Forgiveness is not:	Forgiveness is:
Agreeing to trust an untrustworthy person.	Being willing (when appropriate) to allow the offender to rebuild responsible trust.
Passively tolerating future abuse.	Exercising disciplinary measures with redemptive intent.

Misunderstanding #1
Forgiveness Means Dismissing Moral Responsibility

Some people try to deal with their bitterness by resorting to a form of popular determinism. The offender commits hurtful acts. Some do not want to hold them responsible. They seek to excuse the offender by saying that the offender is the victim of other people and circumstances. If we can convince ourselves that our offenders could not help what they did, we may not have to face the pain of the offense and the responsibility to forgive. This is a way of playing the ostrich; keeping our heads in the sand instead of dealing with the problem.

God's word agrees that our environment can influence us, but there is a crucial difference between influence and determinism. Christians have a basis for genuine empathy for even those who commit wrong. Because of the Fall, all of us have an inner inclination towards evil that makes us susceptible to external temptation. I experienced this in my own family when in 2006, just after my wife and I had returned from Jerusalem, one of our daughters wrote us as follows:

My dearest one, by the time you will be reading this note, I would have been far away from home. I am so sorry I am writing, it's just because I cannot face you to tell you that which I am about to write. I don't deserve either of you in this family. You all had me in mind when you spoke constantly about my relationship with ___, but I never listened until things got so bad. I had always tried to end the relationship, but

I could not. The day I finally decided to do so. I changed the turn of my life. After speaking and agreeing and ending everything, I lost the courage and strength to resist that which happened; I tried to get all things out of my mind and forgive myself but it took a while and when I finally did, I thought everything was okay, but I was wrong. I never saw any sign. I never felt anything and even when I fell off a bike nothing happened to me.

The day I went to the hospital to get the wound treated, the doctor decided to do a scan and I was dismayed to discover that I was pregnant. My immediate thought was to run out so as to get hit by a car and just die on the spot, but I thought God had forgiven me so I did not know the reason for the great punishment. Another thought came and that was to get an abortion. I got a doctor and the money to pay, and I was to come back the next day. That night, I had a dream, and all the scenes from just a little sin came back fresh to my mind. Then the next morning, I decided not to go to the doctor. I have to go away so that people do not get to find out. I have made a terrible mistake in my life, but I have forgiven myself and have asked God to forgive me. I need to be away so people would not insult this family because of me. You all do not deserve it. I do not know if I would live but I would be glad even in death to know that you all have forgiven me because I have failed you.

When I read this letter, I cried openly for over an hour before my family members. After that, I realized that I could have wound up in a state of anger and bitterness if not for the grace of God. How would I have responded to my daughter's dilemma if I were in her shoes? As I reflected on those thoughtful and apparently genuinely remorseful words for her sin, my heart went out to her with compassion. Yet I realized that she was still responsible for the results of her actions.

I was shocked then to hear the comment of a church member who said,

> This girl is different than you and me. We could never have
> done what she did being a clergyman's daughter. She could
> have hidden it or aborted.

These words betrayed not only a lack of compassion but also a self-righteous blindness to the wickedness of the heart of this church member. Empathy and compassion must stop short of determinism. I identified with my daughter during moments of trial and brokenness, because I too am a morally good man saved by grace alone (Ephesians 2:8-9), but this does not remove her responsibility for what she did. At some level, her will was operative in all of her actions, and she came under the increasing influence of yielding to temptation because she chose to turn away from what she knew was right. To decide that she was not responsible for her actions creates an endless sequence of victims (including the person who made her pregnant). Such thinking reduces human beings to mere robots, completely programmed by their environment and therefore incapable of God's love.

Forgiveness from the heart always insists on moral responsibility by transferring the right of retribution to the one to whom this rightfully belongs. When I forgive an offender, I do not decide he could not help doing what he did to me. Rather, I decided that it is not my place to pay him back. God alone has this right because all sin is, first of all, an act of rebellion against Him. He is the only competent moral judge who has paid the price for all sins committed past, present, and future. In transferring this crime to a higher court, I am not overturning justice. I am cooperating with God's perfect justice.

Misunderstanding #2

Forgiving is Primarily an Emotion

Many intense feelings may accompany forgiveness. Tender compassion may replace rage; desiring reconciliation replaces cold alienation. Just as bitterness poisons our emotional lives, forgiving will affect them positively. God's spirit is able to open our eyes so that we view our offenders with His mercy. He is able to cleanse our hearts so that they go out to our offenders with a desire for their good. Genuine forgiveness is a miracle of God's grace that affects our emotional lives.

The Bible describes forgiveness primarily as a choice based on the truth, not a feeling. God does not say He "feels" merciful, but that He "shows" mercy. So the one offended must choose against his feelings and decide to surrender his right of revenge. This is the only consistent response for a wicked sinner who has received God's forgiveness. You likewise choose against your feelings when you serve your offender in love. Indeed, God must empower you. He promises to do it as you turn to Him prayerfully trusting in obedience.

Most positive emotional changes are associated with the result of choosing to forgive people. If you withhold forgiveness from your offender until you feel warm towards him, you will probably wait forever. In addition, the change in your feelings towards your offender may be gradual. This doesn't necessarily mean you have not forgiven. It may mean that your emotions haven't caught up with your choice yet. Actions are many reliable indicators. Am I turning away from negative thoughts that emerge in my mind? Am I refusing to follow through with hurtful words and actions? Am I choosing to pray for him and treat him with appropriate kindness? Your offender should become precious in your eyes as human lives in which their love has scope to give (Ephesians 4:28).

Misunderstanding #3
Forgiving is a Once-And-For-All Event
Have you ever decided to forgive someone, and then later realized you needed to forgive him again? Many people conclude that this is the

original idea of forgiving that is inauthentic. If they had really forgiven, their forgiveness would have been once-and-for-all. Although man's forgiveness should be like God's forgiveness, man's forgiveness is always limited. God knows the extent of our sins when He forgives us. Sometimes, we learn more about the extent of our offender's sins against us. A rape victim may learn that her infertility is a consequence of her offender's physical abuse. This new knowledge necessitates a decision to forgive on a deeper level. The point here is that, although forgiveness is a choice, in many cases it looks more like an on-going process something we need to do only once. Rather than engaging in introspection about the genuineness of our original choice to forgive, we will do better if we choose to forgive again, and then move forward in our walk with God.

Misunderstanding #4
Forgiving is Forgetting the Offense

Many Christians think that "forgive and forget" is the only genuine way to really forgive someone. They think you won't ever recall how an offender sinned against you. If you do think about it, this is the proof that you never really forgave him.

This is an erroneous view of forgiving derived from misinterpreting Jeremiah 31:34. God says, "For I will forgive their wickedness and will remember their sins no more." The point here is not that God erases our offenses and forgives us unconditionally. God being omniscient knows everything, and disciplines Christians out of His loving concern for their good. The discipline presupposes that he takes note of our sins. However, once we ask Him to forgive, God will never again count those sins against us. He will never use them as a basis for condemning or rejecting us. He has fully satisfied his righteous wrath against our sins through the death of Christ (I John 2:2).

Forgiving from the heart means waiving the right of focusing on past offenses as an excuse for hating the offender and plotting revenge. It also means choosing not to use the offenses against the person in the future as reminders, gossip, and other forms of retaliation. The offenders' offenses may reoccur to you at times, but the motivation for doing so will not be retributive. Smedes wrote,

> The act of forgiving, by itself, is a wonderfully simple act; but it always happens inside a storm of complex emotions. It is the hardest trick in the whole of personal relationships. ... We forgive in four stages [hurt, hate, healing, and the coming together]. If we can travel through all four, we achieve the climax of reconciliation.[5]

Roger wrote,

> If you ever had your feelings hurt and you forgave the person for it, and, inside of you, you allowed them the chance to hurt your feelings again, then you really did forgive them. You entered into real, true forgiveness because you allowed them the opportunity to come back to you again. That's forgiveness. But if you remember who they were and what they said and what they did and the time they did it, and if you say you forgave them, you didn't. We don't really forgive when we still have the feeling of the memory of the hurt.[6]

What do you expect to experience about your forgiven memory offenses? The answer is you have laid down the right to pay the person back so you will not purposefully recall and ruminate over the offenses committed against you.

---

[5] L.B. Smedes, *Forgive and Forget: Healing the Hurts We Don't Deserve* (New York: Pocket Books, 1984), 18.

[6] J. Roger, *Forgiveness: The Key to the Kingdom* (Los Angeles: Mandeville, 1994), 27.

In general, therefore, it will play a smaller and smaller role in your thinking and life. It does not mean your memories of the offenses will not emerge into your mind. Various events (conversations, dreams and related memories) may trigger your memory, sometimes with alarming emotional intensity. When this happens, you should not focus on the fact that you remembered the offense or experienced negative emotions in your memory. Rather, you focus on how you will respond to what your memory recalls. There is no reason to beat yourself for recalling an offense over which you do not have control, because you are not created as a robot. The best thing to do is to confront it with the memory of God's forgiveness. Then you use the memory of God's forgiveness as the basis for your choice to forgive your offender. Above all choose to move forward by setting your mind on something that is true and good (Philippians 4:8).

Misunderstanding #5
Forgiving Means Trusting an Untrustworthy Person

Many people are unwilling to forgive their offenders because they think forgiving is synonymous with trust. If you forgive someone, does it mean you must trust him even if he remains untrustworthy? Does forgiving a sexual offender mean that you entrust your young female children to his care? Does forgiving a church member who is a thief mean that you allow him to handle collections? Does forgiving someone's dishonesty means that you go on believing everything he says?

Forgiving relates to past offenses. It chooses to accept the painful consequences and sets the offender free from retribution. Forgiving, therefore, is something we choose to grant freely, with no strings attached. Trust, however, relates to the present. It is a measure of the confidence we have in a person's reliability. Trust is earned. This is precisely why we speak of people being "trustworthy." They have proven themselves to be worthy of our trust in an area because of their reliable performance. Trusting an untrustworthy person is not spiritual. It is foolish, and you may get burned. It is irresponsible, and others may be injured. It is unloving when you refuse to discipline the offender.

It is possible and common to grant someone forgiveness from the heart while still insisting that he or she earns back your trust. Those who insist on being trusted just as they admitted their sins are suspicious because they would probably not grant this request if they were in the other person's shoes. After confessing that he had been a weak district leader for years, one former district leader asked his other church leaders to forgive him. They did, but they did not trust him with responsibility for a long time afterwards. Flanigan buttresses this, saying,

> Forgiveness is the method by which people in intimate relationships let each other 'off the hook' for various acts of ruthlessness and unkindness. ... It occurs in a transaction, [and] is the method by which the wounded person can readmit an outcast, [and] the wounded person reopens his heart to take in and reaccept his offender. ... When it is final, it imparts peace to the forgiver and restores a modicum of kindness to the human community as a whole. ... Forgiveness is the accomplishment of mastery over a wound. ... It is the process through which an injured person first fights off, then embraces, then conquers a situation that has nearly destroyed him. Forgiveness is also a gift given to the self. ... Once received, the gift of forgiveness releases an injured person from the burdens and shackles of hate. Forgiveness is the ultimate liberator. ... Forgiveness is a journey; and a journey is a process. ... The process of forgiving begins at its point of departure, **naming the injury**, and ends at its destination, **the emergence of a new self.** It is

> the stopping-off points in between are **claiming the injury,
> blaming the injurer, balancing the scales,** and **choosing
> to forgive.** ... To choose to forgive means making the choice
> to release the injurer from debt, making the choice to cut the
> bonds that still hold you to the injurer, [and] making the choice
> to look ahead, not back.[7]

The district leader's initial immature response was outrage. He ganged up with pastors at the lower level to rebel against the leadership of the district. After all, he was genuinely sorry for his behaviour. He was telling them the truth. Upon reflection, however, he realized they could gauge his heart only by his actions, and his actions rightfully told them he was untrustworthy. The leaders' mistrust was valid. Although not a perfect principle of resolving conflict, it teaches the lesson to place greater value on their trust. The author is sure that this former district leader will not abandon his work and go to school without permission in future if given a second chance for leadership. When people betray trust they may be forgiven freely but we become irresponsible if we restore them to the previous responsibilities immediately. We give time until repentance and they have shown a proven record of reliability.

Forgiving from the heart is different from trust, but it often involves the willingness to allow the offender to rebuild trust by showing responsibility. Forgiving from the heart keeps its eyes open, but it desires to see the restoration of the relationship. After getting burned, we may decide never to trust offenders again in any area, no matter what they do to change. At this point, the refusal to trust has probably become retributive.

---

[7]B. Flanigan, *Forgiving the Unforgivable: Overcoming the Bitter Legacy of Intimate Wounds* (New York: McMillian, 1992), 2, 5, 11, 71-72, 145.

Misunderstanding #6
Forgiving Means Passively Tolerating Future Injury

Some Christians view forgiveness as adopting a dormant posture toward an offender. The idea of placing charges on a physically abusive spouse, for example, seems to some people incompatible with extending forgiveness. Since forgiving from the heart means not paying people back, doesn't this mean we should not make our offenders experience any negative consequences for their sins? Many people are quick to foster this view so they can go on preying on others, but such a view is a serious distortion of forgiving from the heart.

Forgiving from the heart is an expression of love, and the love that extends forgiveness also disciplines. It is willing to confront offenders to help them to experience the natural consequences of their sins and to creatively devise consequences to influence their lives for good. Jesus chose to give himself to his captors because it was God's will for him to die for our sins, but He never allowed people to run over him because they wanted to. He had "love" of the rich young ruler, but also exposed the ruler's idolatrous love of money (Mark 10:21; Revelation 3:19).

He told the Laodicean's "Those whom I love, I rebuke and discipline. So be earnest and repent." Paul says,

> Do not repay anyone evil for evil ... do not take revenge, my friends, but leave room for God's wrath ... do not be overcome by evil, but overcome evil with good.

Nevertheless, He goes on to inform Christians that civil government is "God's servant, an agent of wrath to bring punishment on wrongdoers" (Romans 12:19-22; 13:4). God forbids vengeance and the taking of personal bitterness, but He encourages Christians to resort to credible police officers to protect them from thieves. While some people use the civil authorities to take vengeance on their enemies, Christians can seek to follow the steps of restoration outlined by Jesus in Matthew 18, including excommunication when other lesser disciplines have failed.

Misunderstanding #7
Forgiving is Similar to Reconciliation

Authentic forgiveness is often viewed as the mutual recognition through which repentance is seen to be genuine and right relationships are achieved. By this forgiveness is a synonym for reconciliation. Laying down the right to take retribution and re-assuming the responsibility to love are the first steps towards forgiveness, but until both parties have resolved their issues, repented of their sins, and restored their relationship, forgiveness has not occurred and reconciliation has not yet happened.

While this view is commendable for its emphasis on restoring estranged relationships, it is incorrect. Reconciliation is the restoration of relationships when both parties have resolved the enmity that separated them. It is always bilateral. Both parties must be willing to reconcile a broken relationship. Most divorcees know through painful experience that a partner who is willing to forgive and work on the marriage is not enough to ensure its success until both of them agree to do so.

In contrast, forgiving from the heart is a unilateral decision to release an offender from retribution. It is forgiving others regardless of whether they ever repent or agree to work on their relationships with us.

Reconciliation is usually a product of forgiving from the heart, and forgiving from the heart is a condition for reconciliation. However, they are not the same thing. Paul makes this distinction in the way God deals with us. He says through Christ's death, God extended forgiveness to all people ("not counting their sins against them"), even to those who are non-Christians. He then goes on to appeal to those who have yet to receive this forgiveness to "be reconciled to God," (II Corinthians 2:19, 5:20). Because God has extended forgiveness, reconciliation is possible, but it does not occur unless we first choose to receive his forgiveness, and thereby become reunited with Him. If we choose to continue in rebellion against Him, we deny His forgiveness in our lives. Thus, we remain separated from God and justly under his judgment.

Claiming, therefore, to have forgiven someone from your heart, yet having no desire to be reconciled with the person calls into question the genuineness of the forgiveness you profess. There are, of course, times when reconciliation proves to be impossible. I just pointed out above that a case of divorce resolves a breakdown in relationships but it fails to bring reconciliation. We live in a fallen world, where relationships sometimes break beyond repair. Physical death can also permanently prevent reconciliation. By God's grace, however, we can forgive even those people and move forward in our walk as a result. Indeed, if your reticence is due to his refusal to repent, your position may be justified. In this case, you may simply be saying that you refuse to act as though the issue is resolved when it is not. However, if you are unwilling to consider reconciliation of any sort regardless of his demonstrated repentance, you may have deceived yourself about having forgiven the person.

Discussion Questions

1. What are some causes of the broken relationships between groups that occur because of unforgiveness?
2. What are some of the unresolved soured relationships in your church, your village or among your neighbours in the city?
3. Are there any prejudices you have inherited about members of your family, spouse, church, and another group in your community?
4. Can you think of any evidence that show these prejudices are true?
5. Why is it difficult to live as Christians in the midst of sour relationships?

CHAPTER 4

FORGIVING

Is it Possible?

Are Christians obliged to forgive unrepentant people? While God's forgiveness of man is a subject many theologians have written about; interpersonal forgiveness appears to be relatively neglected. While there are many books on interpersonal forgiveness, it is rare to find a careful exposition of the biblical model of forgiveness. This is a critical matter. Scripture warns those who withhold forgiveness from others that God does not forgive the unforgiving! This is not an insignificant theological statement. Who wants to risk being unforgiven by God? I was preaching in my church one Sunday on the subject of interpersonal relationships with those who hurt us. As I was walking out of the church, a young man asked me whether it is normal to forgive a person immediately after he or she commits an offense against him? It was a great question about the conditions required for interpersonal forgiveness.

Conditions for Interpersonal Forgiveness

There is some theological debate about these conditions. Generally, those who share reformed theological convictions agree on how people should forgive one another. However, there are differences of opinion.

Many godly people who have contributed immensely to psychology and biblical counselling disagree. The main point of their disagreement concerns the conditions required for interpersonal forgiveness. There appear to be four options. Some argue Christians should forgive personal offenses immediately and unconditionally. Others contend that it is better to forgive only people who repent. Thirdly, others argue for both depending on the situation. Finally, there are those who argue that different kinds of forgiveness have different requirements.

Kinds of Interpersonal Forgiveness

Over many years of working with people I have come to identify two kinds of forgiveness: heart forgiveness and verbal forgiveness. Heart forgiveness is expressed unconditionally. Verbal forgiveness is expressed conditionally. Failure to understand this has caused serious confusion among Christians. In heart forgiveness, it is a battle. In verbal forgiveness, it is a response. Heart forgiving is the battle of the soul to subdue the reaction of the flesh to the point of injury. Verbal forgiveness is the response of the forgiving heart to repentance to repentance of the offender.

Generally, Christians who only recognize one kind of forgiveness - verbal forgiveness - agree that bitterness is overcome in the heart. They do not refer to heart-work as forgiveness. However, both my theological training and experience lead me to believe that it is appropriate to call heart-work "forgiveness." Indeed, this is the kind of forgiveness that Christ demands from his followers. For even when offenders do not repent of their actions, Christians are required by the Bible to forgive the offender's personal offenses.

To understand the differences between the heart and verbal forgiveness, we need to carefully delineate the terms. Here are some ways through which the reader may understand these differences.

- First, they differ in direction. Heart forgiving is directed towards God. With the help of God, the victim seeks to set aside bitterness, hatred, and revenge. Verbal forgiveness is directed towards man. The victim responds to the repentant offender telling him that he is forgiven.

- Second, they differ in what they accomplish. Heart forgiveness restores the victim. It removes the evil thoughts that undermine communion and fellowship with God. Verbal forgiveness restores the offender. It renews fellowship and makes full reconciliation possible.

- Third, they differ in what is required. Heart forgiveness is the required response to all personal offense. Verbal forgiveness is required only when the offender repents.

- Fourth, they differ in location. Heart forgiveness can be done alone before God in prayer. Verbal forgiveness must be communicated to the offender.

- Fifth, they differ in possibility. Heart forgiveness is the response of the offended party, so it is always doable. The victim does not need the cooperation of the offender. Verbal forgiveness requires the repentance of the offender, so it is not always doable.

- Sixth, they differ in finality. Heart forgiveness must be done continually. A man might sooner tame the wind than still the recurring bad memories that ignite bitterness. Yet as often as he remembers, he must forgive. Verbal forgiveness is required only once. Yet the victim may need to reassure the offender of forgiveness. The man who verbally forgives yet nurses a grudge has not truly forgiven.

Christ's Command to Forgive from the Heart

Christ's command to forgive sets no general limiting conditions. Though heart forgiveness and verbal forgiveness differ, they both are aimed at people. One area of confusion is that the Christians are required to forgive. This is seen in the Lord's Prayer. In Matthew 6:12-15, the Christian is commanded to forgive all debtors. Debtors are not just those who owe money, but those who offended in any way. Not only must the Christian forgive debtors, but all debtors. Thus Matthew writes:

> And forgive us our sins for we ourselves also forgive everyone who is indebted to us.
>
> —Luke 11:4

In Mark 11:25 we are to forgive everyone who is indebted to us without exception.

> Whenever you stand to pray, forgive if you have anything against anyone so that your father who is in heaven will also forgive you your transgressions.

To gain a clear understanding of Mark, we must compare it with Luke 17:3-4,

> Be on your guard! If your brother sins, rebuke him, and if he repents, forgive him. And if he sins against you seven times a day, and returns to you seven times saying, "I repent," forgive him.

I believe, therefore, that the kind of forgiveness spoken of in Mark 11:25 is different from that of Luke 17:3-4. The forgiveness mentioned in Mark is to be granted unconditionally and unilaterally (done by one person only). The forgiveness in Luke, however, is a response to an offender, requiring the cooperation of both the offender and the offended.

Thus, sins are forgiven in two ways. If anyone injures me, when I set aside any feelings of revenge, do not cease to love him, and even repay him with benefits instead of injuries, I show forgiveness. For the Lord bids us wish our enemies well. He does not demand that we approve of what He condemns, but only wishes our minds to be purged of hatred.

The second kind of forgiving is when we receive a brother in such a way as to think well of him and be convinced that the memory of his fault is wiped out before God. The distinction here is between the kind of personal forgiveness where hatred is set aside in the heart, and the interpersonal forgiveness in which a brother is received back into fellowship.

Luke 17:3 equally describes both kinds of forgiveness. You are commanded, upon his repentance, to forgive him. Forget the injury and never think of it again (much less upbraid him with it). Though he does not repent, you must not bear malice toward him, nor meditate revenge. However, if he does not at least say that he repents, you are not bound to be as free and familiar with him as you have been. Mark 11:25 clarifies that when we are in prayer, we must remember to pray for others, particularly for our enemies, and those that have wronged us. Now we cannot pray sincerely that God would do them good and wish them well, if we bear malice toward them. If we have injured others before we pray, we must go a nearer way to work, and must immediately from our hearts forgive them.[1]

Thus I believe that the heart of forgiveness is internal forgiveness, which is opposed to external forgiveness. We forgive by forgiving in our hearts whether the person ever gets right in their life or not. That is internal forgiveness. Later on, when they have restored themselves and things have been made right, we give them that external kind of forgiveness that makes the relationship all that it

---

[1]David W Augsburger, *The Freedom of Forgiveness*, (Chicago: Moody Press, 1988), 28.

should be. Forgiveness is to be an attitude of the mind as part of having the mind of Christ.

The Consequences of Disobedience

Not only should the Christians forgive all offenders, but there are penalties if forgiveness is withheld. "If you do not forgive, neither will your Father who is in heaven forgive your transgressions" (Mark 11:26). The Christian who refuses to forgive must face the fact that, in some sense, God will not forgive him. By this, I do not mean to say that the Christian can lose salvation. Franzmann writes "Forgiveness and the disciple must need to live by it in relation to his fellowman."[2]

Nevertheless, the person is subject to temporal penalties. Failure to forgive brings the disciplining hand of God. It hinders fellowship, intimacy, and communion with God. In the worst case, just as with any continuous sin, continuous failure to forgive may indicate that the person is not really a Christian at all that the person is not truly brought into God's kingdom. Either way, it is hard to imagine a situation more serious or perilous by not experiencing God's forgiveness. Anyone who seeks loopholes in the command to forgive all debtors or who would teach others to withhold forgiveness should soberly and fearfully consider the severity of the penalty. So how do we put into practice Christ's command to forgive?

Practicing Christ's Command to Forgive

I pointed out earlier that heart forgiveness requires the release of the offender. Forgiving from the heart is graciously responding towards the offender. Forgiveness is the act in which an injured party allows the party responsible for the injury to go free. The release that occurs

---

[2]Martin H. Franzmann, *Concordia Self-Study Commentary* (Saint Louis: Concordia Publishing House, 1979), 21.

in heart forgiveness does not necessarily imply reconciliation with the offender. It is not condoning their action. What after the victim seeks is to find peace. Forgiveness creates that inner peace by not blaming the offender, but by taking one's life experience less seriously and changing the grievance to a story. Forgiving from the heart includes the following:

1.   Acknowledging a wrong has occurred
2.   Recognizing that a wrongful act creates an obligation for repayment.
3.   Choosing to release the offender from that obligation and for the victim to cover the loss.

Morris writes, "The verb *charizomai* in a sense of forgiving [is used] mostly to bring out the truth that Christians ought to be forgiven people."[3]

The release is expressed by no longer requiring the offender to repay demands for compensation. Using Ewell's words, the idea of forgiveness is found in either religious or social relations and means giving up resentment or claim to requital.[4] The biblical emphasis on release is consistent with the contemporary understanding of forgiveness. Webster writes,

> People are said to forgive when they 'cease to feel resentment
> against' [an offender] when they give up resentment to claim
> to requital [and] when they grant relief from payment.[5]

---

[3]L. Morris, "Forgiveness," *Dictionary of Paul and His Letters* edited Gerald F. Hawthorne, (Downers Grove, Illinois: Intervarsity Press, 1993), 312.

[4]Walter A. Elwell, *Evangelical Dictionary of Theology*, (Grand Rapids, Michigan: Baker Book House Company, 1984, 2000), 460.

[5]*Noah Webster's New Twentieth Dictionary of the English Language* Unabridged Second Edition, (USA: William Collins Publishers, 1979), 720. Requital and repayment are

How can the Christian know that he has forgiven his offenders? I realized from my own experience that true forgiveness occurs when we refuse any thoughts of revenge, when we do not cause our enemies' mischief, when we grieve during their calamities, and pray for them. We must seek reconciliation with them where possible, and show ourselves ready on all occasions to help them. To be genuine, forgiveness should come from the heart. Certainly, when the offender repents, the Christian should verbally forgive him. Nevertheless, this means nothing unless the Christian has already forgiven from the heart. The heart is important because the Bible says it is the centre of personality. The heart is the seat of the intellect, of the will, and of feelings, and it is the battleground for all decisions. In modern thinking, the heart is associated mainly with the emotions. However, in the Bible, the heart was not separated from the intellect. Bright writes,

> Unless you are willing to walk in the light, you will never know the truth; unless you are willing to walk in the light, you will never see the light.[6]
>
> —John 7:17

It is the heart, not the hand, that rules the body, and it is in the heart that Christ dwells.

Biblical Clarification on Mending Relationships

A Christian is to distinguish between forgiving an offender face-to-face and God's forgiveness. Jesus instructed,

---

similar. Requital is demanding something in return, compensation, or retaliation. When the offender is released, the claim to requital and repayment is set aside.

[6]Bill Bright, *Handbook of Concepts for Christian Living*, (Jos, Nigeria: GCM, 2010), 46.

> If your brother sins, admonish him, and if he repents, forgive
> him. If he sins against you seven times a day, and seven times
> comes back to you and say, "I repent," forgive him.
>
> —Luke 17:3,4

God wants us to understand that we are not permitted to set a limit on the number of times we forgive an offender who asks for our forgiveness. God requires us to grant an offender immediate forgiveness in our hearts, whether or not he ever asks for forgiveness. When we refuse to do this, we allow a root of bitterness to grow up in our hearts. Bitterness will defile our lives and the lives of other people as well. Do not say you are not in a position to tell offenders that you forgive them unless they first ask for your forgiveness. God has not authorised us to do this. This may lead sinners to think that they are "off the hook." Unrepentant offenders are not off the hook with God and depending upon the nature of the offense, they may not be off the hook with the legal authorities. So how can a Christian become sure of obeying the Lord's command concerning forgiveness?

Support from Scripture

The Bible provides clarification on the principles of mending relationships in Matthew 18:21-35. The last verse indicates Christ's requirements needed for forgiveness. The Christian is expected to always forgive from the heart. Carson writes, "It is possible for one party to forgive another from the heart while the other party remains hardened in self-righteous bitterness."[7] Forgiveness may occur along with reconciliation, but in other contexts, forgiveness may also simply reflect the stance of the one who forgives, even though no reconciliation with the other party has taken place.

---

[7]David A. Carson, *Love in Hard Places*, (New York: Cross-Way Books, 2012), 13.

There is an apparent absence of the offender in Matthew 18:35, as well as in the Lord's Prayer, and in Mark 11:25-26. Heart forgiveness paves the way for verbal forgiveness. If the Christian has truly forgiven from the heart, he responds appropriately to an offender's repentance. He will seek reconciliation where possible. He will confront and rebuke not just for his own benefit, but also out of love for the offender. Even if the offender does not repent, if the Christian still forgives from the heart, he has satisfied Christ's command to forgive.

Different Opinion on Forgiveness

Some people opposed the idea of heart forgiveness. They think there is no forgiveness without repentance. Scott claims there is no forgiveness before the offender's repentance, writing "The full restoration of a sinning brother [occurs when] he is now repentant."[8] This example shows that forgiveness is modelled after God's forgiveness and is unmistakably based on repentance and faith. Therefore, Scott believes forgiveness must not be granted to those who do not seek repentance. If the person repents, forgive him (Luke 17:3). The one who has something against another may not continue to hold it against him in his heart. Yet, forgiving in prayer does not preclude his responsibility to pursue the matter with the offender. Thus, heart forgiveness occurs synchronously with verbal forgiveness.

Others think that when you say "I forgive you" to a person, you make a promise to him. You promise not to remember his sins by not bringing it up to him, or to yourself. The sin is buried. However, the offender has to be involved. Otherwise, he is not forgiven by not repenting to the one he offended. To this end, forgiveness is not a decision that we can make without the person who wronged us being aware of it. This opinion does not believe anyone can obtain

---

[8]John Scott, *The Contemporary Christian*, (Leicester: Intervarsity Press, 1992), 24.

forgiveness from his heart activity alone. Rather, it must be a two-party agreement.

I disagree with those holding to this view. God has provided a means for handling the multitude of offenses that we commit against one another through the death and resurrection of Jesus Christ (1 Peter 4:8). Quoting Proverbs 17:9, Peter points out loving one another "covers a multitude of sins." If God forgives us unconditionally, why would the believer not forgive another person unconditionally? MacArthur writes, "Small offenses or small sins do not require forgiveness."[9] But it is a grievous theological fallacy to say all petty offenses are overlooked as not forgiven. God forgives all sins whether small or big (Psalms 103:3, 12). "How blessed is he whose transgression is forgiven, whose sins are covered" (Psalms 32:1). Covering someone else's sin is the very essence of God's forgiveness. God provides unconditional forgiveness.

We ought to release our sinful bitterness and hatred whether the offender ever seeks it or not. If the offender repents, we are prepared to complete the process by saying, "I forgive you." Miller writes, "A Christian is not only [simply] to have an attitude of forgiveness or spirit of forgiveness."[10] The essence of running a marathon is not the prize at the end, but the struggle to endure the race. Forgiveness is not the fruit of a forgiving attitude, but rather the struggle of the heart is recognized in Proverbs 18:19. A brother's offense is harder to be won than a strong city, and contentions are like the bars of a citadel. This struggle occurs early in Scripture. It is seen in Cain's bitterness against God. It is also displayed in his jealousy against his brother Abel. God

---

[9] John MacArthur, *The Freedom and Power of Forgiveness* (USA: Cross Road Books, 2009), 27.

[10] Wendell Miller, *Forgiveness: The Power and the Puzzles* (New York: Clear Books Publishers, 1994), 67.

told Cain, "Sin is crouching at the door, and its desire is for you, but you must master it" (Genesis 4:7).

Heart forgiveness is analogous to a high school wrestling match. Try to picture the wrestling match that takes place in the heart. The flesh responds to injury by challenging the regenerated will. It longs for the takedown with bitterness, revenge, and rage. The will rises to subdue the flesh and arm it with faith and Scripture and the will manoeuvres to find a weakness. The flesh fails, the will is on top, the flesh is pinned against the floor and the countdown begins. However, the greater the injury, the greater is the strength of the flesh. Before the countdown is finished, the flesh rises and the will crashes against the floor. It tries to stand, but the flesh prevails with its arsenal of pride, personal honour, and the demand for vengeance. Anger is skilfully deployed, and the will falls down. Now the flesh is on top. Urgently, the will cries out to God for wisdom, and God answers. Renewed humility makes way for the power from above. Demands for justice are handed over to God, and a weight is lifted. Now, with renewed strength, the will rises to subdue and pin the flesh. The countdown is over. Victorious, but wounded and exhausted, the will rests. Let it rest, for there will be another battle. The flesh will rise again. However, when it does, there will be sufficient grace to fight it. People of God, this is what it means to forgive with the heart. It is more than an attitude, and it is more than a willingness to forgive. It is the on-going struggle of the will to overcome the bitterness of the flesh. This is what the writer means when preaching, teaching, and writing about forgiving from the heart.

Does Heart Forgiveness Prevent Church Discipline?

Another objection with respect to heart forgiveness as a type of forgiveness relates to church discipline. MacArthur writes,

> If forgiveness were unconditional, then this entire process of discipline would be impossible. It is my contention that the very existence of such a program as this requires us to believe that forgiveness is conditional.[11]

In contrast I would argue that forgiveness connected with church discipline is conditional, but heart forgiveness is unconditional. Since heart forgiveness is often confused with verbal forgiveness, heart forgiveness is also confused with forgiveness associated with church discipline.

Church discipline is another type of verbal forgiveness. It requires repentance, and it requires confrontation. However, the Bible says woe to an elder or church member that fails to forgive from the heart before confronting. If he has not already forgiven the erring brother from his heart, he will run the risk of further alienating him. The Christian is admonished to forgive the erring church member from his heart, prior to his repentance. Nevertheless, no forgiveness should be verbally expressed until the erring brother actually repents. There are similar issues in family discipline. How many parents unnecessarily provoke their children because they discipline them in anger? Can children see the face of love through a parent's wrath? Let parents be diligent to forgive from their hearts before they raise the rod. As it is written, "Fathers, do not provoke your children to anger; but bring them up in the discipline and instruction of the Lord" (Ephesians 6:4).

---

[11]MacArthur, *The Freedom and Power of Forgiveness*, 35.

Does Heart Forgiveness Eliminate the Need for Confronting?

There are many occasions when it is necessary to confront people for their own good. Simply overlooking an offense will harm them. The Bible says open rebuke is better than secret love (Proverbs 27:5). Does this mean that forgiveness must be withheld? In church discipline, heart forgiveness is unconditionally given, but verbal forgiveness is delayed until the offender repents. Would this be true with any kind of confrontation that involves an offense? Whether or not the offender responds to confrontation by coming to repentance, should forgiving from the heart take place?

MacArthur writes "There are times when it is necessary to confront an offender. In such cases, unconditional forgiveness is not an option."[12] However, I am convinced that heart forgiveness is the unconditional act of forgiveness that God provides for Christians.

God's people are like Christ and like Stephen. We are to forgive at once every sin, regardless of who the sinner is and whether he repents or not. Do people understand this? We are not to hold any grudge against a person who has wronged us, no matter how much they have offended us and or how deeply we are hurt.

Is Heart Forgiveness Different from How God Forgives?

Some people object to heart forgiveness as a kind of forgiveness, thinking it differs from the way God forgives. They say that since God does not forgive a person unless he or she repents, a Christian should not either.

---

[12]MacArthur, *The Freedom and Power of Forgiveness*, 35.

There are problems, however, when people make such baseless comparisons with God's forgiveness. God is the judge and regenerates His people before He forgives them. We do not have such power. God is perfect and has never needed a human's forgiveness. God knew mankind would fall in Genesis 3 ahead of time, so He planned for man's salvation. Forgiveness existed in the mind of God before the heavens and the earth were created (John 3:16).

Does Heart Forgiveness Ignore Human Effort?

Some agree that heart forgiveness is required. However, they throw up their hands in frustration saying, "I can't do this! This is for super Christians. This is not something that I can do." Remember Paul says, "I can do everything through him who gives me strength" (Philippians 4:13). People must not give up because the consequences are deadly. Bitterness clogs the lifeline of spiritual health. When that lifeline is clogged, the Christian should look for the obstructions and remove them.

One of the biggest obstructions is our forgetfulness.

1. We forget the magnitude of forgiveness and focus on personal injuries. We overlook our accumulated debt of lifetime sins against God.
2. We forget the cost of forgiveness. The greater the physical and emotional pain, the harder it is to forgive. Unwillingly, we endure the injuries of people but are not willing to forgive them.

Yet, Christ willingly endured the cross so that people might be forgiven. We forget why we are here. Instead of living for the glory of God, we become absorbed with the defence of our own dignity and honour. We forget the humility of Christ. Instead, we seek recognition for ourselves. We forget how God creates holiness so we forget that sovereignty puts difficult people in our lives to refine our grace. We forget the doom of the ungodly. Distracted by their temporary prosperity, we forget that they will soon face the judgment of God. We forget where we go for help. We forget that the God who was with us in salvation is with us in the furnace of injury and affliction, and he is with us to carry us, to teach us, to love us, and to bring us safely home.

Marison speaks sensitively about those for whom the pain of an injury is severe. He writes,

> When entrapping sin is a refusal to forgive, we must be sensitive to the pain and fear that often lie beneath it. We must give support and comfort, encouraging our fellow-disciple to trust his Lord's grace and power: "I can do everything through Christ who gives me strength."[13]

Nevertheless, we must also keep before him the Lord's command. Easy or not, Christ both commands and makes possible forgiving those who offend us, who sin against us, whose faults and failures get under our skin. The Holy Spirit writes this command into our hearts as He confirms to us God's forgiveness, saying "It is for us now to trust and obey" (Proverbs 3:5). In the next chapter, we will see the benefits for forgiving from the heart.

Discussion Questions

1. How can you help reconcile those who fail to forgive each other?
2. Do you have ethnic tensions as a result of unforgiveness in your own church, fellowship, group, or community? Discuss the causes and possible solution.

---

[13]Patrick Marison, *Forgive as the Lord Forgave you*, (New Jersey: P & R, 1987), 45.

3.   Is it right to prepare for future trouble? Can you think of any Scriptures that say you should do this?

CHAPTER 5

BENEFITS OF FORGIVENESS

Cultivating the practice of forgiving is well worth the effort. Sadly, many Christians do not figure out what the benefits of forgiving others are. The writer of Proverbs says:

> Do not be wise in your own eyes; fear the Lord and turn away from evil. It will be healing to your body and refreshment to your bones.
>
> —Proverbs 3:7, 8

> My son, give attention to my words; incline your ear to my sayings. Do not let them depart from your sight; keep them in the midst of your heart; for they are life to those who find them and health to all their body. Watch over your heart with all diligence, for from it flows the springs of life.
>
> —Proverbs 4:20, 22

Forgiving frees a person from the emotional bondage that undermines his effectiveness.

> Therefore, since we are surrounded by such a great cloud of witnesses, let us throw off everything that hinders and the sin that so easily entangles, and let us run with perseverance the race marked out for us.
>
> —Hebrews 12:1

God wants us free from any weight that distracts us from running the race of life. Unconditional forgiveness allows us to throw off everything that hinders and live a Christ-honouring life.

Another benefit is that when one quickly forgives from the heart, he avoids bitterness. Bitterness is a devastating sin that can be directly traced to the failure to forgive. You become irritable when you continually nurse the wound inflicted by another person. Malignant thoughts and harassing memories eventually distort how you look at life. Anger begins to rage and can easily get out of control. As your emotions begin to run wild, your mind may do the same. You entertain desperate ideas for revenge. Even casual conversations with others become your forum for slander, gossip, and vengeance against the offender. Your flesh, that horrible remnant of your old sin nature, has gained control.

There are physical effects too. When a person harbours resentment against someone, certain glands in his or her body (including the pituitary, thyroid, and adrenal glands) produce excessive amounts of hormones. These hormones can cause a breakdown in a person's body. If this is how an unforgiving spirit is, we need to learn to forgive from the heart.

Who Should We Forgive?

Forgiveness is not saying the offense did not matter. Jesus suffered that we might be forgiven, commanded us to forgive, and instructed us on how to forgive. However, He also demonstrated forgiveness with His very life. Consider the way He prayed on the cross,

> Father forgive them, for they do not know what they are doing.'
> And they cast lots, dividing up his garments among themselves.
> —Luke 23:34

Who did Jesus forgive from the cross? Much ink has been spilt on this subject. Some have argued that He only forgave the Romans rather than all His enemies.

Psalm 69:20-28 refers to the suffering of Jesus, and states,

> Reproach has broken, my heart is so sick.
> I looked for sympathy, there was none;
> for comforters, but I found none.
> They also gave me gall for my food
> and for my thirst; they gave me vinegar to drink.
> May their table before them become a snare;
> and when they are in peace, may it become a trap.
> May their eyes grow dim so that they cannot see,
> and make their loins shake continually.
> Pour out your indignation on them,
> and may your burning anger overtake them.
> May their camp be desolate;
> may none dwell in their tents;
> for they have persecuted him
> whom you yourself have smitten,
> and they tell of the pain of
> those whom you have wounded.
> Add iniquity to their iniquity,
> and may they not come into your righteousness.
> May they be blotted out of the book of life
> and may they not be recorded with the righteous.

Jesus knew this passage, and He knew that all Scripture had to be fulfilled through Him. This was fulfilled when Jerusalem was destroyed and when the Jews were persecuted. It is still being fulfilled today among those who are spiritually blind.

So when Jesus prayed, "Father forgive . . . " he was praying for the forgiveness of all His enemies, not just the Romans. Jesus could have cried out like Zechariah, who was stoned for serving the Lord, prayed "May the Lord see and revenge!" (2 Chronicles 24:22b). Carson writes,

> The most important thing about this prayer is not the precise way in which it was answered or the precise degree of guilt that the men incurred and for which they needed forgiveness, but the way it discloses Jesus' heart.[1]

This is still the heart of Christ for us today.

Why is forgiveness apparently a difficult virtue to master? Forgiving others and self are problematic. People need to understand the problem to be able to come up with effective solutions. When this happens, then people can better appreciate the power of forgiveness.

Why the Difficulty in Forgiving Others?

Pride and self-righteousness hinder forgiveness. When we use the faults of others to build ourselves up, the sins committed against us are useful in building our egos by comparing ourselves to others (Luke 17:3-5; 18:9-14; Genesis 3:12-13). When we want to shift attention from our shortcomings, we jump at the chance and point to what others have done wrong. Thus, when we forgive, we forfeit the advantage we sinfully think we possess.

Paying back is perversely sweet considering The story of Absalom taking revenge on his half-brother Amnon for his rape of Absalom's sister Tamar (II Samuel 13:20-29) show that there is a perverse satisfaction from doing so. If we want to hurt those who have hurt us, holding a grudge seems like the perfect way to really make someone pay. "Do unto others what they have done unto us" becomes our perverted rule of conduct.

---

[1]David Carson, *Love in Hard Places* (Wheaton: Cross-Way Books, 2012), 16.

Nevertheless forgiveness rejects revenge. The result of my seeking revenge is that it hurts me. Instead Christ taught us to forgive (Matthew 6:14-15). In the next chapter, we will examine the downward spiral of unforgiveness.

Discussion Questions

1. "Church members who constantly refuse to forgive others usually think they must earn God's acceptance." Discuss this statement.
2. Discuss further the misconceptions about forgiveness looked at in this chapter.
3. Describe what it was like to refuse to forgive someone who offended you.
4. What consequences did you experience? If you forgave that person, what benefits did you experience?

CHAPTER 6

AN UNFORGIVING SPIRIT TAKES TIME TO DEVELOP

An unforgiving spirit does not develop overnight. It is the by-product of angry responses and takes time to come to fruition. Often the following sequence of events characterises the process.

We Get Hurt

The seeds of an unforgiving spirit are planted when we are hurt in some way. It may be a physical, an emotional, or a verbal hurt. It may be a hurt we experienced in childhood or adulthood. It really makes no difference. Since we live in a self-centred world, we often experience our first hurt as children. Unfortunately, early hurt usually comes from people we love and respect the most. Our hurts at times come because of rejection we have experienced. We may not perceive it as rejection initially, but that is what happens when people hurt us. We may feel hurt, pain, abandonment, embarrassment, hatred, or negative emotion. All of these relate to rejection. At this stage of rejection, it usually leads those who feel rejected to confusion because of their bewilderment.

We Become Confused

Often our initial response to hurt, regardless of the form it takes, leads to confusion. We experience a sense of bewilderment, and we are not sure how to respond. It is similar to being in a state of shock. In this stage, we may think that what caused the hurt is not really happening. We may even have a physical reaction to having a deep feeling of emptiness. We may even feel as if we are fasting and hungry. Many people have actually become sick after experiencing rejection. This stage of confusion is usually short-lived, and people move into the third stage of diversion.

We Look for a Diversion

We have discussed that the confused stage usually comes because of pain and as normal human beings; we always endeavour to avoid anything that will bring us pain. When we are hurt emotionally, instead of thinking about it, we tend to find ways of avoiding those painful thoughts, memories, or events. People resort to mental diversion. We both avoid thinking about the situation, and how to address the issues that hurt or cause us pain. Instead, we change the subject when certain topics are brought up. This desire to divert around past hurt motivates some people to drink alcohol heavily. Some go on drugs and become addicted to both prescriptive and non-prescriptive drugs. My older brother was an alcoholic. He was always unable to cope with his life situation, as he constantly felt a sense of rejection even though none of our family rejected him.

When people get hurt and confused, they tend to resort to physical diversion rather than respond in the spiritual dimension. At this stage, they tend to avoid certain people, places, and events. Usually, people who find themselves in this category would avoid anything that reminds them of the hurt. I cannot forget the experience of a pastor's daughter whom I counselled in 1996. She was immersed in a state of bitterness against her father. Discussing her disappointment concerning her broken engagement, I asked what would be her reaction if a pastor proposed the idea of marriage to her. Reacting sharply, "I will never marry a pastor." When I further asked more open-ended questions, I discovered there was truly no connection between her father and any other pastor in West Africa. Nevertheless, in her mind, using the name "pastor" meant rejection. Therefore, pastors were to be avoided at all costs.

Going Around Our Hurts

When we try to go around our hurt without seeking solutions to address them, it becomes very easy to arrange our thought patterns and lives in general towards a wrong direction, instead of turning to Scripture. Some people take this line of action to make them never be exposed to anything that reminds them of their hurt. They make attempts to forget the whole problem ever occurred, yet they find it hard to overcome the action or person who caused them hurt.

We Deny the Problem

The fifth stage is one of denial. I have come across many people who denied they were ever hurt. This phenomenon is very common in the Christian setting in West Africa, especially in Nigeria. They cover up everything bad that happens with them, including their hurts. Many Christian parents have refused to accept their son has got a girl pregnant, or their daughter is expecting out of wedlock. They hide it because of shame, since they are in church leadership or occupy high status positions. This is the devil's deceit at work. Many times in the course of hiding the hurt of a pregnancy out of wedlock, women resort to abortions of innocent children. In certain cases, those who attempted to abort a child have themselves died in the process simply because of shame.

Rather than accepting and treating the problem, they deny it. Many parents whose daughters became pregnant become pretenders. When they meet with the offenders, they smile and say, "I forgave him or her long time ago." I have met with adults and young people who are carrying around a load of bitterness. They exhibit their feelings through their tempers and the way they behave towards members of those families or church members who relate to them. They fail to see a connection between denying the sin ever happened, so their problems are compounded.

Once I attended a strategic planning meeting in South Africa and met a woman who refused to greet any man wanting to say hello to her before the start of each session. After the third day of the Strategic Planning Meeting, I asked the woman why she was behaving this way towards men.[1] It transpired that the woman's problem concerned her relationship with her father. Her father had physically abused her during her adolescent years. She later discovered that her father was the cause of her inability to have children when she was married. Although most people did not know about her past, she became bitter at her father and his sin. However,. she flatly denied she had been abused and, instead of forgiving her father, decided the only solution was to deny what had happened. I had the privilege of counselling this woman while at that meeting, and leading her out of the bondage to an unforgiving spirit and bitterness.

---

[1] I held two International Leadership Positions. One was as the Country Coordinator for African Services Nigeria. This position gave me the opportunity to travel out of Nigeria to attend Strategic Planning Meetings (SPMs) from 1998 through 2001. The other position was when I became the first West African Director for Community Bible Study International.

Another friend referred a church member to me for counselling concerning bitterness toward his father. The church member reluctantly came to see me because he concluded that his problem all through life was his relationship with his father while growing up. The member's struggles in life had less to do with his father's rejection, however, than with his denial of unresolved conflict with his father, and the resulting bitterness it had caused. He wrongly denied the conflict and pretended as if nothing had happened to him. The lesson for everyone is no matter when people deny their hurts and bury them without forgiveness, they will become defeated in their lives, and their behaviour will be affected.

We Become Defeated

Regardless of how successfully people think they have buried their hurts, how is their behaviour affected? They become short-tempered, oversensitive, shy, critical, and jealous as a result of unresolved rejection. The tragedy is when people deny they are harbouring their hurts, they move from place to place while seeking a perfect place where they can eliminate their undesirable behaviour. People can move house, change jobs, change friends, rededicate their lives, make New Year's resolutions and new friends, memorize Scripture, pray long prayers, fast, or undertake any number of spiritual exercises, but still not change inwardly. Until they deal with the root of their problems, they find that the matter is not solved by making new friends. Until they are willing to treat their sickness of bitterness, they will find that making a pilgrimage to Jerusalem is not the cure for their ills. Ultimately, they think that their obtaining peace depends on how busy they are in church activities. Instead, they find themselves becoming defeated in their attempts to look for renewal.

In marriage counselling, frequently wives speak of how their husbands verbally and physically abuse them. Wives describe their husbands' violent and unpredictable tempers. They weep often as they give accounts of how some of these husbands have made their lives and the lives of the children unbearable and miserable. Surprisingly, the offending husbands who are involved in domestic violence often shake their heads in agreement with their wives' accusations. However, such husbands often remain in their failure and defeat in their marital life. I have witnessed some of the emotional breakdown and cries of pain wives encounter. In many counselling sessions, one thinks that as the couple walks out, there has been a "life-changing" meeting. Yet, in spite of this, some of the offending husbands continue with the same behaviour they exhibited before the counselling. Why? Although they may say sorry for their actions and deeds, they did not deal with the root problem.

On the other hand, I have witnessed results in counselling where husbands and wives dealt with their anger and the hurt they had been carrying for years, and exposed and forsook their bitterness. They finally renounced their ugly tempers and buried them under the cross of forgiveness. I have witnessed situations where men and women have laid down their unrealistic expectations of their wives and husbands forever. Those quick turnarounds came about after their roots of bitterness were discovered, acknowledged, and dealt with. People who fail to dig into the root causes of their bitterness often become discouraged.

We Become Discouraged

This is the critical stage. It is usually the stage where people seek either professional or biblical help to bail them out of their circumstances. It is the level though which seems to be hopeless for some people. They think the problem will never change or their circumstances will never get better. Once there is any new distrust, it shatters the peace initiative that had begun. The new incident confirms and adds to the suspicion of the parties; with the result that both think the conflict cannot be resolved!

It is normally during this stage that some husbands leave their wives. This is because they think either their wives will not change, or they are unable to rekindle their first "loving feelings." Like the Laodicea church members, they are neither cold nor hot (Revelation 3:15; 16). Their love for their wives has become lukewarm. Similarly, at this stage women who had stopped drinking alcohol (in obedience to the Lord), will begin to depend on alcohol again as well as prescribed drugs to make it through the day.

Once a couple advances to this stage, it becomes dangerous and it makes it easier to resort to an unforgiving spirit. It could also lead the couple where their mutual respect is destroyed. If it is allowed to go unchecked, it can dissolve the loyalty and unity of purpose that hold a marriage together during difficult times. Extramarital affairs become a viable option for some people who have publicly spoken out against adultery. Divorce becomes a real option for couples who unconditionally pledged lifetime vows. Those who do not foresee and deal with this discouragement begin to believe there are no better circumstances in this life. Those same people often choose to escape it by taking their own lives (suicide).

We Discover the Truth

The truth is that it is not how a person starts in one's spiritual life that matters; it is how strongly they finish. Finishing strong does not mean finishing perfectly. Some who finished strong were previously involved in sexual immorality (for example, David in 2 Samuel 11-12).

Some who finished strong waited until late in life to surrender to their Creator and Saviour. Some who finished strong were considered at mid-life to be utter failures. Some who finished strong found they were frustrated and disappointed by situations not of their own making. Some who finished strong overcame personal failures and major setbacks by embracing the grace of God. On the other hand, some who do not hit the finishing line strong have chosen to remove themselves from the Lord's protection and power. Readers need to know that we do not finish strong by focusing on where the finishing line is. We finish strong by fixing our eyes on Jesus (Psalms 37:23-25, Hebrews 12:1-2). The spiritual life requires self-discipline. This has helped many people in life. Many people whom the author has talked with testify of the positive effect when they discipline themselves by dealing with bitterness.

I have learned that self-discipline means the effort to create space in which God can act. It means preventing everything in one's life from being filled up. In one's spiritual life, self-discipline means to create space in which something can happen that you had not planned or counted. In choosing forgiveness, the offender obtains mercy through someone's help by God's grace to discover the root of bitterness. When this action takes place, we gain insight into why we act the way we did. We are able to identify the connection between the past and the present. Then we allow the pieces to finally fit together to enable the offended person take responsibility.

We Take Responsibility

This stage is intended to help people own up to their responsibilities. They decide to quit blaming others. They decide to quit waiting for everybody and everything else around them to change. They open their hearts for God to have His way regardless of how it might hurt. Once people reach this level in their search for forgiveness, they are likely to experience deliverance.

The following true story illustrates the point. A Christian vendor brought charges against a Medicine Store for refusing to pay a significant part of his fees. The Medicine Store's accountant/ Chief Financial Officer claimed that she had paid all appropriate amounts according to their lawyer's interpretation of the contract. The two parties were more than two hundred million Naira apart.[2] They requested a Christian arbitrator to judge the matter in accordance with the Scripture (1 Corinthians 6:1-8) rather than go to court by filing a lawsuit. The vendor and the accountant claimed that there were no personal issues to reconcile. From both of their views, they only disagreed over the interpretation of the contract and asked for help in resolving the matter.

The coordinator encouraged both sides to seek first to resolve their dispute through mediation so that the opportunity for reconciling the difference could be realized.

Mediation differs from arbitration in that an impartial mediator facilitates negotiation of material issues, as well as bridging of personal issues, through mutual resolution that could lead to confession and forgiveness. The parties retain all rights to settle their own disputes and reach an agreement. As both sides presented their stories, the mediator helps them to identify both personal and material issues. The mediator reminds them of Christ's love and forgiveness of their sins, and he admonishes them to respond to God's love in their actions towards one another in order to move towards a resolution.

In arbitration, the parties give up their right to make their own decisions, and they empower the arbitrator to act as a judge who hears both sides' stories and issues a binding decision. In such settings,

---

[2]About U.S.$560,000 in April 2018.

the parties are much less likely to admit personal fault or forgive their opponent, because they attempt to convince the arbitrator of the rightness of their positions. In addition, an arbitrator cannot decide issues of the heart. For example, he cannot issue a decision to force a party to confess sin, forgive sin, or show love. He can only preside over judgment on substantive issues.

The vendor and the accountant for the Medicine Store reluctantly agreed to try mediation, provided that the mediator could later be appointed as their arbitrator and issue a decision for them if they were unable to reach a voluntary settlement. I was eventually appointed their mediator/arbitrator.

The mediation took almost thirteen hours. We spent the first eleven hours addressing personal issues that they had claimed did not exist. The moment the vendor and the accountant resolved their personal issues through mutual confession and forgiveness, they were able to arrive at an agreement quickly on the two hundred million Naira difference in ninety-five minutes. After they forgave each other, their stored trust and respect for one another made negotiation on the material issues much easier. Arbitration was not needed. Taking responsibility caused them to resolve their conflict and made restoring relationships a reality. The two parties were satisfied with the settlement. The vendor and the accountant rejoiced over the restoration of their personal relationship. As they celebrated the victory they earned over their hurts, other people around them glorified Christ, giving God the glory that they had experienced God's forgiveness through Christ.

The above story about the vendor and the accountant showed that both of them claimed that their dispute was simply a misunderstanding of their oral and written agreements. Neither of them had admitted that personal relationship issues were involved. Yet, we spent a considerable amount dealing with those personal issues that they said did not exist.

When the dispute first emerged, it might be correct to define it as a misunderstanding in contract interpretation. However, when the conflict deepened and emotions increased, sinful desires led them to sinful words and actions.

What had actually happened was that the vendor had become defensive and persisted in contacting the accountant. The accountant had quickly tired of what she perceived to be petty complaints, and instructed her assistants to take messages whenever the vendor called. The vendor became angry and began to attack the accountant's assistant with an accusation against the accountant. When the assistant became frustrated at being caught in the middle, the accountant directed that the vendor's calls be transferred to other departmental heads. Then, in a management meeting, the accountant announced her judgment of the vendor's behaviour as unchristian. The vendor became aware that his phone calls were being transferred around and of the accountant's warnings to her fellow workers. In turn the vendor responded by telling other clients about the ungodly behaviour exhibited by top officials of this well-known organization.

Follow the progression in this story. The misunderstanding led these two wonderful Christians to respond to their disagreement in sinful ways. It landed them into denial, avoidance, and aggressively attacking each other, rather than speaking to each other honestly and owning up to their responsibilities. In their efforts and zeal to serve their own interests, they sought to bring hurt to the other person.

However, when they were given the opportunity to express their personal hurts, the vendor and the accountant began to understand how they had sinned against God and against one another. Their "undisclosed anger" against one another prevented them from resolving their dispute because they no longer trusted each other. Taking responsibility for the sin issues helped them to rebuild confidence, and trust allowed them to resolve their financial disagreement. Both the vendor and the accountant were delivered from holding onto bitterness by taking the responsibility in dealing with their sins. This is the biblical model that is needed for forgiveness among people living under unresolved conflicts as a result of broken relationships.

We are Delivered

How does one define deliverance? Elwell writes,

> Deliverance embraces safety and escape. It means to cover, to bear, take away, to pardon and is used for both divine forgiveness and human forgiveness.[3]
>   —Psalm 18:50; 44:4; Judges 15:18; I Kings 5:11; 13:17; II
>   Chronicles 11:14

The prophets announced that the future deliverance of the nation from various perils would result from God's protective power (Joel 2:32; Obadiah 17). In the New Testament, deliverance involved the idea of being released, liberated from some evil situation such as torture (Hebrews 11:35) or bondage (Luke 4:18).

The final outcome for those of us who are willing to deal with an unforgiving spirit is deliverance. My friend, you can be free of that embarrassing, inappropriate, family-splitting behaviour. You say, "But you do not know what has happened to me. You do not know what I have been through." You are right. Nevertheless, the author has known people who have been delivered and restored from all sorts of life situations. Jesus forgives and you are called to forgive others.

------

[3]*Evangelical Dictionary of Theology* Second Edition (Grand Rapids, Michigan: Baker Academic, 2007), 460.

He poured out His life to forgive and free us from death. Forgiveness wipes and cleans the junk that holds us back. It brings into focus a life filled with hope and happiness. Forgiveness is important and essential in all aspects of our lives. As God rules your heart, there is no limit to this beautiful and powerful gift. Forgiveness is all about relationships, so we should treat it like conversion in our social, church, business communication, and transactions. Forgiveness is a choice.

Forgiveness as choice helps us to wake up in the morning without planning to hurt others. As a choice, we ask were there words spoken that deeply hurt the person I love? As a choice, did you cause someone injury with your tongue? As a choice, did you feel guilty about an event that ended in someone's death? Guilt is a heavy weight to carry. Self-hatred can consume you like a raging brushfire. Remember the roadblocks to forgiveness are obvious, including pride, selfishness, and unwillingness to admit you are wrong.

We can be vindictive and vengeful if we do not seek forgiveness. God knows where you are at and seeks to restore you to a wonderful relationship with Him. Though you may feel beaten down, remember there is a way to joy and peace. As a choice, ask God to take away your resentment and bitterness. Be real and tell Him what breaks your heart. The power is in His forgiveness. Forgiveness as a choice has a dimension in controlling anger.

Discussion Questions

1. Where is the place of the Holy Spirit in a Christian life when he or she fails to forgive?
2. How do you practice forgiveness when resolving broken relationships between Sunday school children?
3. What if you thought you had forgiven someone, only to discover that you still resent them, resentment that you can neither figure out, nor let go of?
4. How can you handle the residual sadness and anger that come up even after you thought you have truly forgiven someone?
5. What factors would you consider in deciding whether to practice forbearance with or angrily confront an offender?

CHAPTER 7

OVERCOMING ANGER TO FORGIVE

I have discussed forgiveness in detail and now turn to the lesson on anger because it helps a great deal in handling those who hurt us. In this chapter I hope to provide guidelines for overcoming anger by being patient, tolerant, and slow to get angry. We will discuss relevant passages on the subject of anger, deal with the results of anger, and the thoughts that motivate anger, plus how to battle against and control anger. Let me begin with an illustration that is very familiar in the African context.

A story was told about a tiger who woke up one morning and felt great. He felt very good, and he went out, cornered a small monkey, and roared at him, "Who is the most powerful animal of all the African animals?" The poor little monkey replied, "You are, of course. No one is mightier than you." A little while later, the tiger confronted a wildebeest and bellowed, "Who is the greatest and strongest of all the animals?" The wildebeest shook so hard. It could barely speak, but managed to stammer, "Oh great tiger, you are by far the mightiest animal in the jungle." Seeing he was doing well, the tiger swaggered up to an elephant who was quietly munching on some weeds. The tiger roared at the top of his voice, "Who is the mightiest of all the jungle animals?" The elephant grabbed the tiger with his trunk, lifted him up, slammed him down, picked him up again, shook him until the tiger was just a blur of orange and black, and threw him violently into a nearby tree. The tiger staggered to his feet, looked at the elephant, and said, "Man, just because you do not know the answer, you do not have to get so mad." Friend, we can laugh at the expression of the tiger in this story, but uncontrolled anger can be a disaster. An example of such is the story of King Saul in the Bible.

King Saul was a tall man. In fact, he stood head and shoulders above everyone else in Israel. Unfortunately, as impressive as Saul's height was, he had another characteristic that was even more remarkable, his temper. Saul's volcanic anger first erupted onto the pages of Scripture after David's victory over Goliath. As the men returned from battle, the women greeted them with this improvised song, "Saul has slain his thousands and David his tens of thousands" (1 Samuel 18:6-9). Bitter jealousy gripped Saul's heart, and he became "very angry." He flew into a rage at being unfavourably compared to a perceived rival. The next day, Saul was toying with a spear while David was playing his harp before the throne.

Saul suddenly straightened and flung the spear at David with all his might, trying to skewer him. Saul's resentment toward David led him to do this, not once but twice. So volatile was Saul's temper, David had to devise intricate ways of discovering Saul's state of mind before he dared risk eating a meal at the royal table. When he found out that his own son was part of this message system, Saul grew so furious that he had a go at Jonathan with the spear as well. After these initial blasts of anger, King Saul spent the rest of his reign chasing David across the hills of Palestine, a hound after a particularly elusive fox. Saul's anger left his kingdom, his family, and his relationship with his most able soldier (David) in shambles. That is how anger is. It is destructive.

That is also true of a scenario that happened in the Nigerian Senate. In July 2016, in the media, Senator Dino Melaye from Kogi State allegedly boasted angrily, saying "I would beat up a Senator from Lagos State Mrs. Oluremi Tinubu and impregnate her without any consequences." Anger led him to vomit careless words. It is also true of a husband and father who "pulls the trigger" when his wife or children irritate him. Anger destroys. You have seen the impact of your anger the last time you lost your temper. You discovered the truth of Proverbs, "A brother offended is harder to be won than a strong city" (Proverbs 18:19).

Now you want to change. Anger has become a habit like breathing; you do not even think about it. Perhaps your habit is to be as mild mannered as the tiger's super ego, yet there are some people who push your button, and off you blast into orbit. Can you change? It will take some hard, Spirit-directed work, but you can change (Galatians 5:16-23). Walk by the Spirit, and you will not carry out the desire of the flesh (Galatians 5:16). God has given us the resources through the Holy Spirit to overcome anger. However, how do you go about walking by the Spirit? How can you begin to exercise the fruit of the Spirit that is self-control? (Galatians 5:23). How can you overcome anger and be patient, tolerant, and slow to anger? The first step is to realize the tragic outcome of anger.

Tragic Outcome of Anger

The writer of Proverbs frowns at anger. He speaks of six tragic outcomes of anger. The first is that "a quick-tempered man acts foolishly" (Proverbs 14:17). More directly stated, that means, "Anger makes a person do stupid things." I had a neighbour who had to wear a finger splint for two months because he broke a knuckle when he punched a wall in a fit of rage. A quick-tempered man acts foolishly.

Bitterness is just as bad as murder (Proverbs 14:17). We once read of a man who resented his divorced wife so much that he sent her away empty handed, hoping that the worst would happen to her. Both explosive (punch the wall) and resentful (a person going to get back at someone) reactions are signs that your anger makes you do foolish things. Probably, one of the most dramatic demonstrations of foolish anger we have ever heard of happened on a golf course. A man was so angry at missing a shot that he slashed his club at a tree in frustration. The head of the club sheared off and rebounded from the tree, and the jagged end severed his jugular vein, killing him in seconds. Sin has its own punishment.

Next to foolishness, a second tragic outcome of anger is found in Proverbs 25:28. "Like a city that is broken into and without walls, is a man who has no control over his spirit." Anger allows you to be manipulated by others. Solomon's illustration was of a city whose protecting walls had been breached by a besieging army. Once a hole was punched through the defences, the whole city was levelled. According to Solomon, a person who does not control his temper is equally exposed to being dominated by others. His defences are down. He is not thinking clearly. He is easily conquered.

One can recall an example of this from playing table tennis. There was a senior we often played against who had a tendency to get angry at himself when he made a mistake. Although he was a better player than we were, we knew that if we could get him to bounce the ball off his table or miss an easy shot, he would get angry at himself. When that happened, he would begin to press too hard and make more mistakes. Eventually, he would get so upset he would be a liability to his team rather than an asset. His absence of self-control opened him to being controlled by another. When angry on the table tennis court, he was like a city without walls.

A third tragic outcome of anger in Proverbs is strife. Contention, quarrels, resentment, and bruised feelings follow anger like a shadow. "A hot-tempered man stirs up strife" (Proverbs 15:18). The scent of a pure perfume lingers wherever the person who sprays it leaves. In the same way, wherever a hot-tempered man goes, the odour of strife is sure to follow. His wife, children, co-workers, and friends all know that when he comes around, you can expect a battle or an outburst.

A fourth tragic outcome of anger is habit-forming. It says, "A man of great anger will bear the penalty, for if you rescue him, you will only have to do it again" (Proverbs 19:19). Anger leads to more anger. The angry man will have to be rescued repeatedly. The angry man gets in the habit of responding with outbursts of bitterness. Soon he is in a groove. Any disagreement or disappointment sets him off.

The world has missed this point all together. Psychology (even the self-labelled "Christian" psychology) often promotes catharsis as the solution to anger. The word "catharsis" comes from the Greek word for cleansing. In catharsis, a person is encouraged to "clean out" or get rid of their anger in a furious outburst. For example, the psychologist might encourage the counselee to punch, kick, shout, and even scream obscenities at an object such as a pillow, imagining it to be the person who has offended him. The assumption behind catharsis is that this outburst will empty the anger stored up inside a person. Once the anger has been drained out, it will be gone for good.

That might sound logical, but it is totally unbiblical. First, the outburst of anger is sin, even if directed at a pillow. In the second place, the Bible says, "Be kind to one another, tender-hearted, forgiving each other" (Ephesians 4:32). Raging at someone (even someone who is not there physically) can hardly be called tender-hearted and forgiving. Third, the concept of catharsis completely misunderstands the nature of sin. Far from releasing wrath, the outburst of anger only builds a habit of rage. The surge of hostility might temporarily make a person feel better. However, all the secular psychologist has done is given the sinner practice at responding to personal offenses in an ungodly way. What is shared in the psychologist's office will spill out of his heart in situations beyond the counselling room door.

Let us discuss a fifth tragic outcome of anger. "An anger man stirs up strife, and a hot-tempered man abounds in transgression" (Proverbs 29:22). We have already mentioned that anger brings strife. Consider how the second line of this verse pushes the thought even further. The issue is no longer just strife, but transgression of every kind is now in view. Not only does anger produce strife and more anger, it produces a host of other sins as well. One example is the story of two brothers who blew up at each other at a family reunion. They spoke harshly. They shouted lies back and forth at each other. When they got home, each gossiped by telephone with the rest of the family about the other brother. Gossip turned to slander. Lies were spread in greedy hopes of cutting the other brother out of his inheritance. Add it all up and what do you have? Anger is never a lonely sin. Hot-tempered people abound in transgression.

The last tragic outcome of anger is that it gives Satan control of our lives. "Do not let the sun go down on your anger, and do not give the devil an opportunity" (Ephesians 4:26-27). The original Greek says, "Do not give the devil a place." A bitter heart is Satan's toehold. He will work his evil claws into the division caused by bitterness. He will twist, pry, and push, widening the breach. The devil works his destructive schemes from the perch of bitterness.

Anger's outcomes are tragic. It left Saul's mind, family, and kingdom in a shambles. It will do the same for anybody. When you are angry, you say and do things you normally would not do. Anger gives birth to strife, more anger, and a host of other sins and it is Satan's playground.

That is the motivation to overcome anger! However, a question to ask is what causes hostile anger?

Understanding Hostile Anger

Some years ago, those visiting the museum in Jos, Nigeria may well have seen a puppet display. If they watched the Bight of Benin sculpture while facing the wild animals in the zoo, they may have noticed a jointed puppet controlled from above by string.

Normally sinners want to be in control. Therefore, we bristle at being compared to a puppet, except when it comes to anger. We usually respond in anger as if we were a puppet unavoidably responding to someone's string pulling by saying "He made me angry" or "It is just my nature to debate" or "I am just tired."[1] Other people, our personality, our circumstances - are they the puppet masters that pull the strings, forcing us to jerk and dance in anger? Where does anger really come from?

Discovering and facing up to the hostile source of anger is one of the keys to overcoming anger. Look in the mirror, and you will see the source of your anger. You have heard all the same excuses—such things as salaries are not paid, hormonal fluctuations, killing of a first-class chief, or a bad day at the office. However, the fact is that those things do not force us to get angry. "But each one is tempted when he is carried away and enticed by his *own lust*," (James 1:14, my emphasis). We try to deflect the pain of conscience by blaming our anger on God the Creator on other people. However, James cuts off our excuses just as a kink

---

[1] I have observed the difference between popular and biblical terminology highlights our desire to avoid personal responsibility for our sin. You hear someone saying, "he or she lost his or her temper," meaning anger accidentally slipped out while they were not looking. They were not to blame. Biblical terminology is found in the original language of Proverbs 29:11: "A fool always sends out his spirit." That means you made a choice to get angry.

in a hosepipe cuts off water. Each one is tempted by his own lusts or desires. In other words, you saw the source of your anger in the mirror this morning when you were brushing your teeth. Anger is a choice. Sometimes anger is such a habit, no conscious process of choosing is evident. It has become an automatic response. Yet, nonetheless, anger is a choice to pursue our desires in an ungodly manner.

Consider a typical marriage drama. Abdul calls Amina an "airhead" because she forgot to pay their loan with First Bank Nigeria. Now they will have to pay interest on the amount they borrowed. Does Amina have to respond by calling Abdul "stupid"? She does not have to. It might be easy to follow her lusts and do so, but she could choose to ask his forgiveness for her carelessness, refusing to return insult for insult. It would not be easy, but she could. If exercising the self- control of the Spirit, she will. We are not forced to anger by genetics, circumstances, or people; we choose it. Amazingly, there is great hope in the discovery that you are to blame for your anger and not everyone else. If you are a puppet bouncing and dancing by other people or circumstances, you will never overcome anger. Why not? You have no control over them. If they really do dictate your responses, you will be their anger slave, their marionette-puppet, for the rest of your life.

However, if you are the hostile source of your anger as God says, it is another matter. You can change. What you chose to do yesterday, by God's grace, you can choose not to do today. No matter how insulted, embarrassed, or inconvenienced, you can choose to respond with self-control. Look in the mirror. The real source of your anger is right in front of you. Once you stop pointing fingers at everyone or everything else, you will see it is true. Each one is tempted by his own lusts. Do not be discouraged. Recently, our plumber could not fix a leak until he found the offending pipe. We have found the pipe—your choices and response. Now fix the leak.

You Have the Right!

Why do we become angry? What thinking lies behind the sin of anger? Typically, we burst out in wrath or burn with resentment because we believe our rights have been trampled. Anger is a response, usually revenge for violated "rights."[2] When you believe that your "right" to control your schedule, your personal belongings, or the destiny of your children has been violated, you strike back with anger. When you believe your rights to good health, peace and quiet, fast service, success, or compliments from your spouse have been violated, you fume or plunge into bitterness. Of course, biblically, none of those things are rights. We just imagine they are. Our pride assures us that we deserve children who never disobey, employees who never mess up, and a spouse who can read minds.

You think you deserve never to be cut off on the freeway. Therefore, if you are, you pull beside the offender and shake your fist at the "scum." When we think that we deserve better than what we got, we get angry. We believe our rights have been violated, and we want revenge. Consider the following examples of anger in the Scripture and see if you can pick out the thinking behind them. The first is from the parable of the prodigal son. Which of his "rights" did the older brother believe had been violated?

> Now his older son was in the field, and when he came and approached the house, he heard music and dancing. And he summoned one of the servants and began inquiring what these things could be. And he said to him, "Your brother has come and your father has killed the fattened calf because he has

---

[2]Anger is usually a revenge response. There are exceptions to this. For example, some people use anger merely as a tactic to get what they want. A son knows his Dad does not like to argue, so he flashes anger to avoid having to tell him why he was late getting home from school.

received him back safe and sound." But he became angry and was not willing to go in; and his father came out and began pleading with him. But he answered and said to his father. "Look! For so many years I have been serving you and I have never neglected a command of yours, and yet you have never given me a young goat, so that I might celebrate with my friends."

—Luke 15:25-29

Why did the older brother boil over with resentment? He became angry because he believed he had the right to be spoiled. He believed he had the right to a special celebration. Certainly, he deserved more than his wicked, unworthy brother! To take revenge for his father's "injustice," he skipped the party and pouted. In Genesis, we find another example of anger.

So it came about in the course of time that Cain brought an offering to the LORD of the fruit of the ground. ... And the LORD had regarded for Abel and for his offering. But for Cain and for his offering, He had no regard. So Cain became angry and his countenance fell.

—Genesis 4:3-6

Cain believed he deserved to be accepted by God. When that right was violated, Cain struck out in anger and jealousy against the nearest target, his brother Abel. "Cain rose up against Abel his brother and killed him" (Genesis 4:8). David's oldest brother, Eliab, gives us another example of anger. Eliab believed he had the right never to be embarrassed by his younger brother. Israel was at war, and David had been sent by his father to deliver a care package to his brothers at the battle line.

When he arrived, David heard the taunts of Goliath, and wondered out loud what the reward would be for killing the blasphemous genetic freak from Gath. "What will be done for the man who kills this Philistine and takes away the reproach from Israel?" Now Eliab his oldest brother heard when he spoke to the men; and Eliab's anger burned against David, and he said, "Why have you come down? And with whom have you left those few sheep in the wilderness? I know your insolence and the wickedness of your heart; for you have come down in order to see the battle." But David said, "What have I done now? Was it not just a question?"

—1 Samuel 17:26-29

It is a classic sibling quarrel. A younger brother embarrasses his older brother with dumb questions. The older brother gets angry and insults his younger brother. The younger brother is clueless as to what he did wrong. However, what was the source of Eliab's anger? It was his desire for prestige. He believed he had the right not to be embarrassed by his younger brother.[3]

There other examples we could consider. Balaam got angry and hit his donkey when it inconvenienced him by stopping in the middle of the road. Saul became angry when David threatened his plans for his son to sit on the throne of Israel. What was their thinking in those instances? We have the right to transportation that never inconvenienced us. We have the right for our plans to work out the way we want them to. What do you believe to be your "right"? What sets you off if God, people, or circumstances do not deliver? Think back over the last few things you expect. When you do not get them, it is "torpedoes away!" and heaven help those on the receiving end. We look at impatience in relation to anger.

---

[3]Embarrassment and anger always go together. Take time to think how you respond when your children disobey you in front of the Pastor. They get a double portion of scolding on the way back to the house. Why? The pride of the parent wants revenge for being made to look like a bad family.

Impatience in Relation to Anger

Impatience is a minimizing, excuse-word for anger. All the symptoms and motivations of impatience are the same as anger's, just less dramatic. Sharp words, a resentful glare, a "we deserve better than this" kind of thinking all reflect a lack of patience. Irritation is the child that grows into the adult of anger. Unfortunately, many of the most successful and competent people in our world are also impatient people. Therefore, we tend to excuse impatience. However, here is how God views it. "He who is slow to anger is better than the mighty and he who rules his spirit, than he who captures a city" (Proverbs16:32). The Hebrew language reserved the word "mighty" (*gebor*) for the strongest, most successful, and most capable men in their society. The gebors were the warriors and the wealthy, the movers and the shakers.

However, more important to God than being a person who "gets thing done" is being a person who is patient. "He who is slow to anger is better than the mighty." We believe that what we are doing is so important that no inconvenience should stand in our way. God says nothing is so important that we should exchange patience and self-control for impatient anger. "He who rules his spirit (is better) than he who captures a city." God put a premium on patience. How do you react when you get stuck behind the person who thinks the speed on the highway is twenty rather than one hundred and twenty kilometres per hour?

Be Patient with Everyone

What you should do is remember 1 Thessalonians 5:14-15, which says, "Be patient with everyone. ... Seek after that which is good for one another and for all people." You are not the first one to read that verse with consternation. I am sure Paul's readers in Thessalonica probably did as well. The Greek verb *makrothumeō* (meaning, "to be long to anger") was infrequently used in Greek literature, but in the New Testament it and its derivative (*makrothumía*, "long suffering") are used twenty-two times. In other words, the ancient Greek world was no more inclined toward patience than we are, but Paul said to be patient with everyone. What is that patience like? Here is a useful definition —patience is choosing to suffer long under even painful circumstances without retaliation. Impatience thinks,

> We are so important that no inconvenience should stand in my way. And if you do inconvenience someone, expect a cold reaction, some eye-rolling, frustrated sighs, or finger-tapping retaliation.

It hurts when we put it that way, does it not? Who we are, or what are we doing is so significant that we deserve free-flowing traffic, a copy machine that never breaks, or a child who does not spill his milk.

How can a person overcome impatient anger? Paul gave the solution as he continued in Thessalonians.

> Be patient with everyone. See that no one repays another with evil for evil, but always seek after that which is good for one another and for all people.
>
> —1 Thessalonians 5:14-15

Patience is not retaliating. It is the opposite of repaying with evil (glares, stares, or snorts of disgust). Positively, patience is replacing evil responses with seeking well of a person. Paul's solution to a situation that tests our patience is to guard your response. One should treat well the one who is inconveniencing you. Instead of snarling at a mathematically challenged auditor, friend, wife, or husband, one should give a smile of encouragement. Instead of melting down your wife for being late with supper, ask her how you can help. We should seek after that which is good for one another. Kindness is the replacement for impatient retaliation.

Patience is a choice not to strike back mentally, verbally, or with body language when inconvenienced. Patience is a choice to strike back with kind words and encouragement when inconvenienced. Do not repay with evil. Repay inconvenience with good.

Love and Tolerance

How can you do that? Impatience is a hard habit to break. To begin responding with good to inconvenient people or circumstances, you are going to have to fill your thoughts with two dominant attitudes, love and tolerance. "Love is patient, is not provoked, does not take into account a wrong suffered" (1 Corinthians 13:4-5). Love replaces impatience. One of the hard things my wife endured over the years was my harsh remarks for making us late to church. My wife exhibited patience by learning to tolerate a time-oriented husband. Through her patient and tolerant attitude, I have also learned to tolerate her when there was a reason to be late. Therefore, when your son, daughter, or wife cannot find their Bible and is making you late for church, you can respond with frustration, or you can think, "Love is patient." Love refuses to be provoked by inconvenience or incompetence.

A second attitude that will help you become patient with everyone is tolerance. Paul's epistle to the Colossians gives counsel on how to be tolerant with people.

> As those who have been chosen of God, holy and beloved, put on a heart of compassion, kindness, humility, gentleness and patience; bearing with one another, whoever has a complaint against anyone.
>
> —Colossians 3:12-13

These verses tell humans that patience has lots of companions—namely compassion, kindness, humility, and gentleness. In fact, if you are not patient, it is because you are not on speaking terms with those four companions of patience. Compassion feels sorry for the flustered housewife. Kindness gives her better than she deserves. Humility does not consider a fifteen-second delay to be unacceptable. Gentleness and being principled chooses not to defend its "rights." Phillips translates this quoted passage, "be most patient and tolerant with one another."[4]

Tolerance or forbearance means you choose to suffer long under even painful circumstances without retaliation. Love means you will do it ungrudgingly. Do you remember what fingernails on a chalkboard sound like? Like this sound, you will come across people in life who are just unpleasant. They are blisters on the big toe of life. Sometimes a person you normally get along with will be temporarily insufferable. Circumstances will inconvenience you. Impatient retaliation is the natural response. We do without thinking. Kill it, before the larva of impatience grows into the killer bee of anger. Replace impatient retaliation with unprovoked love and gentle tolerance. This is one of a positive ways to deal with forgiveness when impatient retaliation is replaced with love and gentle tolerance.

Putting off Impatient Retaliation

Under the above heading, it is important to examine a New Testament pattern of what the author understands as putting off impatient retaliation. Paul told the Thessalonians to put off impatient retaliation, and to put on loving tolerance. "See to it that no one repays another with evil for evil, but always seek after that which is good for one another." Retaliation is replaced by its godly opposite, "overcome evil

---

[4]J. B. Philips. *Letters to Young Churches* (New York: Macmillan Company, 1957), 125.

with good" (Romans 12:21) Once you put off impatient retaliation, put on what is always God's plan for overcoming anger.

> You lay aside the old self, which is being corrupted in accordance with the lusts of deceit, and ... be renewed in the spirit of your mind, and put on the new self.
>
> —Ephesians 4:22-24

We can see that Paul applied that plan to overcoming anger at the end of the last chapter of Ephesians. Put off: "Let all bitterness and wrath and anger and clamour and slander be put away from you along with all malice" (Ephesians 4:31). Put on: "Be kind to one another, tender-hearted, forgiving each other, just as God in Christ also has forgiven you" (Ephesians 4:32). Let us continue to apply God's pattern to overcoming anger.

Identifying the Danger of Anger

The initial step toward putting off any sin is to identify the sin. Impatience is a form of anger. Ephesians 4:31 identifies six different forms of anger. Bitterness is the first sin of anger Paul mentions. The Greek word *pikria* referred to the taste left in your mouth by bile or stomach juices. Eventually, *pikria* came to be used of having a bad taste in your mouth toward someone. Bitterness usually comes from brooding. Brooding is what a hen does on her eggs- she sits on them day after day, keeping them warm. Bitterness does the same thing. It broods over the memory of past offenses, real or imagined. Rather than overlooking a transgression, it nurses hurts, keeping them warm rather than letting them die. A bitter person is miserable with anger, hunched over his hoard of slights, griefs, and grudges, secretly counting them by candlelight each night. To counteract hoarded anger, Paul instructs the Ephesians. "Do not let the sun go down on your anger" (4:26). Bitterness is retained anger that is carried over to the next day. It is long-term resentment. Rather than forgive an offense and clear the debt, a bitter person keeps the account open, adding interest daily.

Wrath and anger are the next types of anger mentioned in Ephesians 4:31. Wrath is a momentary outburst, but anger a more sustained response. The words Paul used in the original were the common words for anger in Greek. They covered everything from animosity to fury, from exasperation to rage. Clamour was the next word in Paul's list. This word referred to the raised voices and boisterous shouting of an angry, back-and forth argument.

Clamour is what happens when Nigerian people discuss politics or sports like football. It, at times, leads to red-face shouting. Clamour is what happens when two girls clash over one boyfriend with hostile threats. Clamour is what happens in many homes when mom and dad, parents and teenagers, or brothers and sisters argue with each other. Paul said all arguing is anger that must be put off.[5]

Slander, or evil speaking, was the fifth sin of anger Paul blacklisted in Ephesians 4:31. The Greek word was *blasphemia*. We normally reserve the word "blasphemy" for words that attack God. In Greek, it referred to any hurtful, attacking words. In the context of anger, evil speaking is right on target. Often blasphemia referred to good old-fashioned insults and name-calling. In the gospels, it was used of the crowds "hurling abuse" at Christ during the crucifixion. That kind of verbal mudslinging was what Paul had in mind in Ephesians. Hurtful lies, angry insults, mocking, and name-calling are all categorized under the anger-sin of evil speaking.

---

[5]Some people do not raise their voice when they get angry; they just silence it. They hold onto giving a cold shoulder. The attitude of "I am not-going-to-talk-to-you" resentment is just as much sin as arguing.

Malice was last on Paul's list. This word referred to a desire to cause hurt to another. Malice is what makes a man seek revenge after his girlfriend was told about his other girlfriend. Malice goes out of its way to hurt or upset another. Love seeks the best for another. Malice seeks the worst. Angry malice wants the other person to fail, look foolish, or be wounded emotionally.

More could be said about anger, but Ephesians gives us a good start at identifying sinful anger. However, to overcome the sin of anger, you must identify it in the Scripture and in your life. Do you have a bad taste in your mouth toward anyone, brooding over some past wrong? That is bitterness. Do you get steamed up when your "rights" have been denied? That is wrath and anger. Do you crank up the volume when you disagree with someone in your family or a person at work? That is clamour. Do you insult, name-call, or say untrue, hurtful things when you cannot get your way? That is evil speaking. Do you give a half-hearted, second-rate effort when someone else's plan is implemented? That is malice.

Paul gave us the basic biblical categories of the sin of anger. As usual, identifying the problem is only half the battle. We must still discover anger's godly replacement.

Identifying the Antidote to Anger

We might mistakenly think that anger is overcome by teeth-grinding toleration. We think, "I will stay out of your way if you stay out of mine." Paul said that evil can only be overcome by good, not uneasy neutrality or tight-lipped silence. "Do not be overcome by evil, but overcome evil with good" (Romans 12:21). Following his list of the sins of anger, Paul told the Ephesians that there were three good things that overcome anger: kindness, tender-heartedness, and forgiveness. "Be kind to one another, tender-hearted, forgiving each other, just as

God in Christ also has forgiven you" (Ephesians 4:32). We must put on these holy habits to overcome unholy anger.

Kindness was Paul's first replacement for anger. The Greek word for kindness was occasionally used of clothing and referred to clothes that were easy and comfortable to wear. In other words, you might say kindness is hundred-percent cotton; anger is hundred-percent polyester. A kind person has a soft and relaxed attitude, not a tight, strained, or tense one. The word "kindness" was also used of a drink that had a smooth, pleasant taste. Angry people are antagonistic, rough, and quick to retaliate. A kind person is easy to be around. They are pleasant, relaxed, and comfortable. One of the most important uses of the word "kindness" in the New Testament is in Luke 6:35, which says, "For He [God] is kind to ungrateful and evil men." Kindness is doing loving things for another person, even when he does not deserve it, even if he has been ungrateful and evil. Anger is overcome by the good of kindness. It is choosing to do something pleasant for the one who would normally be the target of revenge. Rather than roasting your husband for getting home late, cook him the best meal possible to welcome him when he does arrive. Rather than blasting your wife for being late with supper, help her by setting the table.

Eusplagnoi is the Greek word for tender-hearted or good-hearted. In Luke 10, the word was used to summarize the Good Samaritan's willingness to use his time, money, and effort to help the beaten stranger. It was also the word used to describe Jesus' attitude toward the lost sheep of Israel. Seeing the people, He felt compassion for them, because they were distressed and dispirited like sheep without a shepherd (Matthew 9:36). When Jesus saw the sin of Israel (the sin he would personally carry on the cross), He did not say, "How could you do this to me? I am going to get even." Instead, Matthew says he "felt compassion for them." Compassion or tender-heartedness views another person's sin as something to be forgiven, not an excuse for anger.

The prodigal's father could have been wrathful and clamorous when his foolish son returned penniless, and he could have said, "How could you do this to me and our family, you worthless son!" However, what was the father's response?

> But while the prodigal son was still a long way off, his father saw him and felt compassion for him, and ran and embraced him and kissed him.
>
> —Luke 15:20

Tender-heartedness concentrates on how the sin hurts the one doing it, not on avenging its offended pride. Tender-heartedness is a reasoned choice to stop the mental rush toward retaliation. It replaces anger with compassionate, selfless concern.

Forgiveness is the third action for overcoming anger. Christians should be "forgiving each other, just as God in Christ also has forgiven you" (Ephesians 4:32). Anger retained past sundown is bitterness (Ephesians 4:26). That kind of anger is overcome by biblical forgiveness. Biblical forgiveness has three basic steps. To eradicate bitter resentment, you must first pursue peace with the person who offended you. Second, where sin was done, it must be repented of and mercifully wiped away. Third, to make sure neither person dwells on what happened, a new and better relationship must be established.

Therefore, kindness is good done to someone who may not deserve it. Tender-heartedness grants compassion rather than retaliation. Forgiveness wipes away a person's offense and puts the whole situation out of its mind. Those are God's replacements for sinful anger. What do they look like in action? In the case of Abdul and Anima, he angrily insulted Amina when she forgot to pay the phone bill. What could he have done to put off anger and put on its good replacement? He could have given Amina a hug of husbandly affirmation and love rather than call her an "airhead." Kindness does well to another, even if she does not deserve it. He could have asked about the pressures that contributed to her forgetfulness. He should have realized that his wife already felt miserable enough about letting down her husband, he could have treated her gently. Tender-heartedness gives understanding and compassion. Abdul also could have overlooked or forgiven her carelessness, putting it out of his mind rather than brooding on it and the extra expense of the interest. It is hard to break anger habits. Like Abdul, you will have to check yourself as you prepare to launch out of the sprinter's blocks of anger and give kindness, understanding, and forgiveness instead. Nevertheless, by God's grace you can do it. Evil can be overcome by good.

Discussion Questions

1. What can I do to overcome a temper problem?
2. How do you plan to control your tongue and restrain bitter words directed at your fellow community members?
3. Does Jesus' parable of the unforgiving servant describe you? How do you plan to respond to offenses in the future?
4. Can you love those who have offended you without holding bitterness against them?
5. How often do you keep a record of wrongs against your spouse, friends, and colleagues in school, community or work?

CHAPTER 8

GUIDELINES FOR BEING SLOW TO ANGER

The Hebrew words that are translated "slow to anger" referring to God, translate the idiom "long nosed." Nobody is quite sure how that idiom came into being. Some suggest the Hebrews saw it this way;when a person becomes angry, their nose became red or burned. God's nose is so long, it never burns up. Whatever the case, we want to imitate God. Eight times in the Old Testament, He is described as being slow to anger. We can learn the secret of being slow to anger by looking at Solomon. Proverbs gives seven guidelines for being slow to anger.

Guideline #1

To be slow to anger, you must first rule your spirit. While we might hail the victorious general, God saves His highest regard for the one who has conquered his temper. The author of Proverbs writes, "He who is slow to anger is better than the mighty, and he who rules his spirit, than he who captures a city [emphasis added]" (Proverbs 16:32).

Any person reading this can comprehend that being slow to anger is ruling your spirit (the inner man). The key to being slow to anger cannot be other people or circumstances. By God's grace, the one thing that a person can dictate in any situation is his response (Galatians

5:22-23).[1] To be slow to anger, a person must rule over his inner man, including his attitudes, thoughts, and responses.

The word "rule" in this verse means to govern, direct, or oversee. To be slow to anger, a person must govern his thoughts and attitudes so that his circumstances and sinful instincts will not. In another place, Proverbs zeroes in on self-control as the key to overcoming anger. It says, "A fool always loses his temper, but a wise man holds it back" (Proverbs 29:11). Literally, it says, "A fool always sends out his spirit, but a wise man calms it down." To overcome anger, you have to make a decision to control yourself, calm yourself down, and not succumb to your anger habit.

There is no trick or secret pill that magically helps you overcome anger. Prayerful dependence on God is, of course, critical. From there, conquering anger is a God-guided choice to respond differently than you want to and kindness rather than anger. The key to killing an anger habit is not changing the people or circumstances around you (James 1:14). There might be some things you can do to limit when you become angry. This can happen when you make no provision for the flesh in regards to its lusts (Romans 13:14). However, the real key to overcoming anger is your application of God's grace to rule your spirit, "calming it down" rather than "sending it out."

Guideline #2

A second principle for being slow to anger is found in Proverbs 22:24-25, which reads,

> Do not associate with a man given to anger, or go with a hot-tempered man, or you will learn his ways and find a snare for yourself.

---

[1]As noted previously, self-control is part of the Holy Spirit's work in every believer's life. That self-control is especially critical in overcoming anger.

This second guideline is not to spend time around someone who gets angry easily. Otherwise, a person will learn his ways. Many things can influence us toward anger, including books or movies with angry characters, friends who are ruled by their temper, and/or television shows where violent actions are the standard response to pressure. Do not be deceived, angry company teaches you to be an angry person.

Guideline #3

The third guideline is to know your enemy. "A stone is heavy and the sand weighty, but the provocation of a fool is heavier than both of them" (Proverbs 27:3). The author of Proverbs shows us that there are some people who provoke us or get under our skin more than others. Here Proverbs notices provocation of a fool. But who is it that provokes you, or what situation sets you off? What is heavier to you than sand and stones? To overcome your anger you will have to know. That is the reason why I call this third guideline, Solomon's admonition to scout your anger.

When a professional soccer team like the Nigerian Super Eagles play in the World Cup, do they show up at the stadium on game day and ask, "Whom are we playing today? Who are their best players? What strategies do they use?" Certainly, they do not. They scout the opposition beforehand, so they are prepared to play against the other side's strengths and weaknesses.

In the same way, you need to scout your anger. Like everyone, you have strengths and weaknesses. There are people or situations that you struggle to handle with self-control. You need to scout your anger, so that you know when, where, and why you usually get angry. Once you have discovered your weaknesses, you can consciously prepare to handle those people or situations with gentleness. For example, I was often sharp and impatient when hungry, or when any member of the family was making us late to leave the house. Knowing that, I try to guard myself against being provoked and impatient all the more closely in those two circumstances.

In the same way, a father who finds that he is often harsh at his children or is grouchy with his wife when he gets home from work, needs to scout his anger. By morning, he is fine. However, when he gets home at six o'clock in the evening, he behaves like a bear. Once, he has "scouted" his anger, he can put special effort into being patient at that time. He can work harder at setting the stress of the day aside before he arrives home. When he walks toward the front door each day, he needs to think, "Okay, I am going to dump the pressure of my job at the front door and be prepared for my family."

"I do not want them to get the backlog of my busy day." By scouting his anger beforehand, he can ask God to help him react with kindness, tender-heartedness, and forgiveness in that situation.[2] Breaking an anger habit takes conscious, direct thought. Whether it is the fool of Proverbs 27:3 that test your self-control or something else, you cannot defeat the enemy of anger until you have scouted it. Once you make effort, you will be far less likely to "send out your spirit." You will be prepared to "calm it down" instead.

Guideline #4

To avoid anger, you must learn to restrain your words. "He who restrains his words has knowledge, and he who has a cool spirit is a man of understanding" (Proverbs 17:27). Words are the kindling of anger. Therefore, one of the most effective ways to avoid anger is to keep

---

[2]His wife can help by giving him some few minutes after welcoming him home to relax, rather than immediately telling him "The food is ready. Can I set the table? The dog's food is finished, etc." Nevertheless, the key to overcoming his anger is still his response, regardless of what happens.

your mouth shut. Every verbal battle (the sin of clamour, Ephesians 4:31) has a point at the outset where it can be avoided. If the verbal flame is lit, it can blow up like a keg of gunpowder. Solomon says, "The beginning of strife is like letting out water, so abandon the quarrel before it breaks out" (Proverbs 17:14).

Just as pinhole leaks in a massive concrete dam can quickly become a rushing torrent, similarly unrestrained words can set off a cataract of anger. To avoid a quarrel, you must see the pressure building and restrain your words. Indeed, restraining your words does not mean clamming up in silent resentment. It does mean, "the heart of the righteous ponders how to answer" (Proverbs 15:28). That verse continues, "But the mouth of the wicked pours out evil things." To overcome anger you must think before you speak. Restrain your words. Ponder your answer so your thoughtless words or, worse yet, your intentional words do not provide wood for the fire.

Guideline #5

The previous guideline was "restrain your words." But what if you have to speak? There are volatile situations in which we must say something. Therefore, Solomon's fifth guideline that we must talk about is to use gentle words. "A gentle answer turns away wrath, but a harsh word stirs up anger" (Proverbs 15:1). Charles Spurgeon once said that when discussing theology, we should use very soft words and very hard arguments. That is a good principle for any conversation. Too often, the opposite is true. Our arguments are soft but our words are hard.

Soft words and gentle answers forestall arguments. Which of the following are examples of soft words that will turn away wrath?

> Can I ask you to turn down the volume on your radio? I am working on our students' grades calculation and I am having trouble concentrating.

Or, "Turn down that noisy thing." A quiet tone and soft words bring calm to potential chaos. In fact, Proverbs 25:15 says, "A soft tongue breaks the bone." To change people's minds, soft words are more effective than a hammer's blows. It was evening time as I continued with writing this section on overcoming anger. Before we ate dinner, our grandchildren who, along with their parents, had come to spend Christmas with us, were playing and shouting all around the house. I was getting frustrated with their shouting and my old nature wanted to let them know in no uncertain terms! But that would not be "slow to anger." Gentile words, controlled volume, and soft tones were hard work, but worth it. At dinner, I had a good relationship with our grandchildren. Solomon said hard words stir up anger. Gentle answers turn away wrath. Use gentle words.

Guideline #6

Here is another crucial guideline for overcoming anger: overlook a transgression. "A man's discretion makes him slow to anger, and it is his glory to overlook a transgression" (Proverbs 19:11). A person of wisdom, insight, or discretion will be hard to provoke. Why? He knows how to overlook a transgression. Now, it is unlikely that Solomon meant wise people completely ignore sin. Proverbs also counsels, "Better is open rebuke than love that is concealed" (Proverbs 27:5). In Matthew 18:15, Jesus commanded believers to help each other by graciously pointing out sin and the need for repentance. Wise people gently rebuke sin because of the good it does for the erring person (see also Galatians 6:1).

If that is the case, then what did Solomon mean when he said the slow to anger "overlook a transgression?" First, the person of discretion does not take offense at the accidental or the inconsequential. The person who is quick to anger takes everything as a personal attack. He acts as if the accident on the freeway was staged for the sole purpose of making him late. Before writing this, I used to think that our youngest daughter purposely waited until thirty minutes before we left for church to get ready, deliberately making us late.. That is a quick-to-anger thinking. Wisdom or discretion does not take offense at the accidental. That is equally true of the inconsequential. They are actions or words that might have been sin, but might not have been. "Was her voice too sharp? Was his tone disrespectful?" The patience of the wise refuses to imagine offenses. It overlooks the inconsequential.

A second way we overlook transgression is by forgiving a transgression. How else does a godly person "overlook" something done against them? He or she forgives the wrong and moves on, wiping clean the chalkboard of the mind. Sometimes on my day off each week, it is hard for me to put the next week's work out of my mind. I get restless and quick to anger. I roam the house, pacing like a caged lion.

My wife knows me well enough not to take those times as a personal attack on her. She extends even more grace than usual to help me relax. If I step across the line of consideration and kindness into sharpness and impatience, she addresses it, forgives me, and overlooks the transgression. She could become bitter or resentful, storing up real or imagined grievances in a mental notebook, but she does not. She knows that the best way to avoid bitterness or an outburst is to overlook transgression by ignoring the accidental or inconsequential and forgiving all of them.

Guideline #7

Generally, anger is retaliation and revenge. If you step on my toe, I return the favour. If your hurt my feelings, I will hurt yours with my words. Therefore, to overcome anger, we must be committed to Solomon's seventh principle. "Vengeance is the Lord's. Do not say, 'I will repay evil,' wait for the Lord, and He will save you" (Proverbs 20:22). Do you wait for the Lord to save you when someone at the office calls you "incompetent," or do you fire off a salvo in revenge? Do you go into deep-freeze mode (the silent treatment) when your spouse says something inconsiderate? Anger is revenge. "You hurt, embarrassed, inconvenienced, or hindered me. You have to pay and I am the collection agency." Vengeance, however, is the business of a just God, not unjust men. "Wait for the Lord, and he will save you."

Here is an arresting thought in the context of anger and vengeance. How many things that you get angry over will God truly take vengeance for? That question shows just how petty most anger really is. Your brother or sister ate the last food, so you respond in anger. Is God really going to take vengeance on so great a sin as eating the last bit of food? How about the unpardonable crime of not straightening the hand towel properly after use? Or not putting the breakable plates in the cabinet in perfectly aligned rows? How petty and selfish is your anger! But suppose someone has really let you have it. They have put your reputation in the paper shredder. They have lied about you and spread malicious rumours. Is it okay to be angry then? "Do not say, I will repay evil; wait for the Lord, and he will save you." Although King David had an area of weakness later after he was king, there was the good part of him before he became king of Israel.

David left a good example of refusing to take revenge even when severely wronged. King Saul chased David all over Palestine, tried to murder him, and outlawed him for no good reason. One day, David had an opportunity to slip a knife in Saul's ribs while the king's guard was down. What a perfect opportunity for sweet revenge! David refused. Later he told Saul, "May the Lord avenge . . . but my hand shall not be against you" (1 Samuel 24:12). David suppressed his lustful eagerness for revenge. By God's grace, so can you. You can wait for the Lord to repay. Embarrassment, inconvenience, or petty grievances can be ignored altogether. Vengeance for real hurts can be left to God. Anger prefers justice. Vengeance, however, is the business of a just God, not unjust men.

Discussion Questions

1. Are you that person who thinks people would ever need counselling if they just loved Jesus enough? Why? And why not?
2. Why does God want us to be quick to listen?
3. Discuss the meaning of listening to find out if listening is the same with hearing?
4. Read James 1: 19-20. Who is James applying this to?
5. What is the consequence of not applying this advice?

CHAPTER 9

YOU CAN FORGIVE AND OVERCOME ANGER

Forgiveness is not saying the offense did not matter. It is not saying we are not hurt by what a person did (Ephesians 4:25). It is not acting as if the event never happened or depended on the offender to apologize first or changing behaviour before they obtain mercy (Romans 5:8). Forgiveness is not letting the offender avoid the consequences of their actions (Romans 13:2). It is not letting the offender hurt us and other innocent people. It does not trust a person again right after they hurt us but requires time to prove their repentant behaviour. Just because we have forgiven someone does not mean that he has changed. Even if he has, our trust in him is broken, and it will take time to rebuild. Bit by bit, as we have good experience with that person we will begin to trust them again. Smedes writes, "The act of forgiving by itself is a wonderfully simple act, but it always happens inside a storm of complex emotions."[1] According to Smedes, "It is the hardest trick in the whole of personal relationships."[2] The understanding here is that

---

[1] L.B. Smedes, *Forgive and Forget: Healing the Hurts We Don't Deserve* (New York: Pocket Books, 1984), 18.
[2] Smedes, 19.

we forgive in four stages [hurt, hate, healing and the coming together). If we can travel through all four, we can achieve the climax of reconciliation.[3]

Forgiving someone means that we recognize that the person has wronged us and we accept the pain their sins have caused us. We bring our pain to the cross and release it to Jesus, and then we will be able to forgive those who hurt us. If we think forgiving is too hard for us to do, we are right. God is the only one who can enable us to forgive. I am not suggesting that forgiving from the heart offers a solution to being unable to forget the hurts offenders have caused us. Like a wounded lion, the scar always remains, even when the wounds have healed. Complete forgiveness from a deep hurt takes time. Forgiveness does not happen all at once. It is like a journey where a person may repeatedly lose his way. A person may start to forgive, but then he may circle back as he remembers the hurt of the offense. Does forgiveness depend on what the other person has done?

Often the human heart is unwilling to forgive until the offender has apologized to them. Jesus, however, provides us with a biblical model for forgiving offenders. His example shows that we need to forgive offenders even when they are not repentant about the evil they have done. After all Jesus died in our place when we are still sinners (Luke 23:34). The biblical model of forgiveness frees us from anger and bitterness and as Christians, if we fail to forgive those who hurt us; we are the people who suffer. Failing to forgive allows Satan a way to prolong anger and bitterness (Ephesians 4:26-27, 2 Corinthians 2:10-11). People can become slaves to anger and bitterness, which can destroy them.

---

[3]Smedes, 20.

In fact, refusing to forgive can make people physically sick by causing headaches, stomach ulcers, or even heart problems. Failing to forgive people makes the unforgiving become as violent and evil as those who have offended them. The good news releases one who forgives from all these. Even further, failing to forgive others can transfer hatred of people onto your children. The habit of not forgiving can result in cycles of revenge and violence that may continue from generation to generation.

Only the practice of forgiving from the heart can break the cycle and commence the healing process in the lives of people who are hurt. We need to know God's forgiveness depends on our forgiving those who offend us. Matthew 6:14-15 teaches, "If you forgive others the wrong they have done to you, our father in heaven will also forgive you. If anyone fails to forgive others, the Father will not forgive them (Mark 11:25). Therefore, forgiveness depends on the Christian understanding of Christ's sacrifice and his or her salvation.

In the same vein, overcoming anger and impatience is a big challenge. Just when you think you have it licked, you will discover "I have the right" thinking in your mind; you will find retaliation in your actions. Do not get discouraged. Just go back and start again. Ask forgiveness. Make a new commitment to rule your spirit. Scout your weaknesses and redouble your defences. What kind of "I deserve" thinking enticed you?

Go back to restraining your words or using gentle words. Remind yourself to look past the accidental and inconsequential with grace. Forgive the consequential with mercy. Give up revenge. By God's grace, you can change! Apply the spiritual lessons from the teaching on the biblical model of forgiveness and overcoming anger so that you can free yourself from the bondage of those who delight to offend you. What has God taught you through reading this book? How would you respond to Him to get you out of the dilemma of harboring bitterness and failing to forgive those you have not released from your heart for years? Where is your timeline that shows that you have been forgiving and releasing people who have offended you from when you were born? As you answer these questions honestly before God, He will show you what specific steps you need to take so that you reap the benefit of a renewed vitality in your relationship with Him and others. What good reason is there for delaying to forgive those who hurt you? Why not begin your practical exercise on forgiveness? Start with the first person on your list whom you have not forgiven. Make a choice to forgive him or her for every painful memory those people have caused.

Stay with that individual until you are sure you dealt with all the remembered pain. After you have forgiven each person for all the offenses that came to your mind, after you have honestly expressed how you feel, conclude the step by praying the prayer below:

> Lord Jesus, I choose not to hold on to my resentment. I ask you to set me free from the bondage of bitterness. I relinquish my right to seek revenge and ask you to heal my damaged emotions. I now ask you to bless those who have hurt me in future just as you have forgiven my past, present, and future sins in Jesus' name. Amen.

Roger leaves us with a conclusion on how we know we have forgiven people in our lives. He writes,

> If you ever had your feelings hurt and you forgive the person for it, and inside of you, you allowed them the chance to hurt your feelings again, then you really did forgive them.[4]

---

[4]J. Roger, *Forgiveness: The Key to the Kingdom* (Los Angeles: Mandeville, 1994), 27.

You entered into real, true forgiveness because you allowed them the opportunity to come back to you again. That is forgiveness.

Discussion Questions

1.   1. What is the evidence that bitterness has put down roots in your life? What reactions might be expressions of that bitterness? Read Ephesians 4:31.
2.   2. Is it possible that the pain caused by your offender(s) might have twisted perspectives in your life about issues you have not fully resolved?
3.   3. Do you fear a similar hurt happening again and then that fear affects your relationship with someone or your neighbour? Is your view of the offender an accurate one? Have you become overly sensitive because of your pain? List some of the ways your view may have been affected.
4.   4. Bitterly responding to an opponent can physically affect a person's body. Sometimes bitterness only show on a person's face. Sometimes it plays a part in the development of chronic illness. Can you think of any physical symptoms in your own life that may be a result of holding on to hurts?
5.   5. Define these terms in your own words: bitterness, wrath, slander and malice. Can you see any evidence of these responses in your life?
6.   6. Bitterness in a marriage relationship can be especially painful and damaging (Colossians 3:19). How might wives also express bitterness toward their husbands?

APPENDIX A

What is Forgiveness?

It is important to begin with a dictionary meaning of the word to forgive. Webster defines that to forgive is "to give up resentment against or the desire to punish, to stop being angry with, to pardon."[1] It conveys the meaning to give up all claims to punish or exert penalty for an offense. Hence, to cancel, or remit, pardon, absolve, and release. Forgiving (adjective) is being inclined to forgive.[2] This means forgiveness is the act of ending resentment, indignation, and anger as a result of a perceived offense. Practically, it means to grant free pardon and to give up all claims on account of an offense and or debt. The practice of forgiveness is expressed between the forgiver and the person being forgiven. At times, forgiveness may be granted without any expectation of restorative justice. That is without any response on the part of the offender.

In another instance, it may be necessary for the offender to offer some form of acknowledgement, apology, or restitution, including asking for forgiveness. Let us now move from the meaning of forgiveness to the contribution of other scholars.

---

[1] Noah Webster, *New Twentieth Century Dictionary of the English Language*, Unabridged Second Edition, (USA: Williams Collins Publishers, 1979), 720.
[2] Webster, 720.

Affinito holds "Forgiveness means deciding not to punish a perceived injustice, taking action on that decision, and experiencing the emotional relief that follows."[3]

Davis offers different approaches to forgiveness from various authors, including Safer's definition,

> Genuine forgiveness demands every mental, moral and spiritual resource you have. ... Nobody forgives spontaneously; victims must make an effort to move beyond their inevitable shock, rage, grief and desire for revenge.

Flanigan also says,

> Forgiveness is the accomplishment of mastery over a wound. It is the process through which an injured person first fights off, then embraces, then conquers a situation that has nearly destroyed him.

Another view defines forgiveness as an "emotion that cannot be generated, forced, or controlled, but which arises spontaneously from within . . . [and] supporters of this perspective often compare forgiveness to love."[4] And yet another view indicates,

> You can't forgive someone who denies that you were injured or who fails to take responsibility for having hurt you. ... In other words, forgiveness without accountability has no teeth.[5]

Davis claims, "on the opposite side of the paradigm linking forgiveness to accountability is the belief that forgiveness should be granted

---

[3]A. G. Affinito, *When to Forgive: A Healing Guide to Help You Come to Terms with Your Emotions* (Oakland: New Harbinger, 1999), 11.

[4]Laura. Davis, *I Thought We Would Never Speak Again: The Road From Establishment to Reconciliation* (New York: HarperCollins, 2002), 268.

[5]Davis, 269.

unilaterally."[6] The last view offered about forgiveness is "resolution [even reconciliation] is possible without forgiveness."[7] Luskin argues,

> Forgiveness is the feeling of peace that emerges as you take your hurt less personally, take responsibility for how you feel, and become a hero instead of a victim in the story you tell.[8]

Luskin believes "Forgiveness is the experience of peacefulness in the present moment. Forgiveness does not change the past, but it changes the present."[9] Forgiveness means that even though you are wounded you choose to hurt and suffer less. Forgiveness means you become a part of the solution. Forgiveness is the understanding that hurt is a normal part of life.[10] According to Luskin,

> Forgiveness is for you and no one else. You can forgive and re-join a relationship or forgive and never speak to the person again.[11]

According to Nelson, forgiveness might help other people, but the primary reason to forgive is that,

> when you forgive, you become human again, no longer "turned to stone." When you forgive, you no longer have "a clenched fist" where your heart belongs. You unburden your heart.[12]

Nelson claims that with practice, forgiveness can become a daily habit, and freedom (from guilt, shame, pain, anger, and the pain of constantly

---

[6]Davis, 274.

[7]Davis, 278.

[8]F. Luskin, *Forgive for God: A Proven Prescription for Health and Happiness* (New York: Harper San Francisco, 2002), 69.

[9]Luskin, 69.

[10]Luskin, 69.

[11]Luskin, 69.

[12]M. B. Nelson, *The Unburdened Heart: 5 Keys to Forgiveness and Freedom* (New York: Harper San Francisco, 2000), 56.

criticizing other people) will be the reward. She does not advocate a particular religious perspective, propose limits or conditions on forgiveness, promise or even propose reconciliation, or see forgiveness as an end in itself. Instead, she explains that unconditional forgiveness, whether inspired by religious beliefs or not, heals. The one who is healed—the forgiver—becomes free from the pain of the past, and is freed to love differently, and love more, in the future. Nelson claims a radical stance:

> Forgive ... regardless of what the other person says or does. Forgive when you're unsure, or afraid, or resentful, or wanting to exact revenge. Forgive when the other person doesn't apologize, or doesn't apologize correctly. Forgive them for that: for their inability, unwillingness, stubbornness, fears.[13]

She cites five keys to forgiveness:

1. awareness—remember who hurt you and how;
2. validation—talks to a sympathetic listener;
3. compassion—strive to see the offender's humanity;
4. humility—reflect on your own faults and failings; and
5. self-forgiveness—opens your heart to yourself.[14]

McCullough, Sandage and Worthington say,

> Forgiveness is an increase in our internal motivation to repair and maintain a relationship after the relationship has been damaged by the hurtful actions of the other person.[15]

---

[13]Nelson, 56.

[14]Nelson, 56.

[15]M. E. McCullough, S. J. Sandage, and E. L. Worthington, *To Forgive Is Human: How to Put Your Past in the Past* (Downer Grove: Intervarsity Press, 1997), 22.

Furthermore, Augsburger writes,

> In forgiving ... perceptions of love must be restored (to love is to perceive another as worthful and precious no matter what the wrongdoing. Wrongdoing is not a valid reason for not loving you). Negotiations of trust must begin until constructive relating is truly achieved.[16]

He claims,

> To forgive there must be the willingness to see another's words and acts as genuinely repentant, to trust the other by risking being wronged again, to be open to relate again in wholesome ways, [and] to venture into new closeness.[17]

Augsburger further notes,

> To receive forgiveness there must be the willingness to affirm my repentance as genuine and to choose to change, to trust my own responses and to risk being freely spontaneous again, to be open again with both candour and with caring, [and] to be close to you without fear.[18]

Casarjian on the one hand holds that forgiveness "is a decision to see beyond the limits of another's personality."[19] It

> is an attitude that implies that you are willing to accept responsibility for your perceptions, realizing that your perceptions are a choice and not an objective fact.[20]

---

[16]D. Augsburger, *Caring Enough To Forgive: True Forgiveness* (Ventura: Regal Books, 1981), 19.

[17]Augsburger, 19.

[18]Augsburger, 19.

[19]R. Casarjian, *Forgiveness: A Bold Choice for a Peaceful Heart* (New York: Bantam Books, 1992), 23.

[20]Casarjian, 24.

Forgiveness "is a process that requires shifting your perceptions again and again ... is rarely a one-time event."[21] Forgiveness

> . . . is a way of life that gradually transforms us from being helpless victims of our circumstances to being powerful and loving co-creators of our reality. Forgiveness is not about what we do, it is about the way we perceive people and circumstances.[22]

Let us now move on to the psychological meaning of forgiveness. This will help us to further understand how forgiving spirit affects human relationships.

Psychological Meaning of Forgiveness

It has not been long the subject of forgiving has gained the attention of psychologists, particularly, social science psychologists. Psychological approaches to the subject of forgiving did not appear until the late nineteenth century. Prior to that time, it was a practice mainly left to Christian care providers. Although there is presently no agreed definition of the meaning of forgiveness in the psychological literature, a consensus has emerged that forgiveness is a process perceived from a behavioural pattern. However, psychological studies show that people who are generally more neurotic, angry, and hostile in life are less likely to forgive another person. Specifically, these people are more likely to avoid their aggressors. They want to take revenge on those who hurt them, even if it is four and a half years after being offended. Yet biblically, people who forgive are happier and healthier than those who hold resentments. The ideas are represented in the writings of certain scholars in the fields of psychology.

For example, J. North—claims forgiveness entails

---

[21]Casarjian, 25.
[22]Casarjian, 30.

> ... the overcoming of negative feelings ... [which] must be the result of an active psychological endeavor on the part of the injured party, even while recognizing that a real injury has been inflicted and that the wrongdoer is to blame for the infliction.[23]

Also forgiveness is *multiperspectival—*

> ... when we forgive another person we have to move from our own perspective, of initial hurt and internal suffering, to that of the wrongdoer, the context of his wrong and his motivation for it as well as his present situation.[24]

> Forgiveness is more than a moral imperative, more than a theological dictum. It is the only means, given our humanness and imperfections, to overcome hate and condemnation and proceed with the business of growing and loving.[25]

The psychology of interpersonal forgiveness, by Enright, Freedman, & Rique explains forgiveness is a

> ...willingness to abandon one's right to resentment, negative judgment, and indifferent behavior toward one who unjustly injured us, while fostering the undeserved qualities of compassion, generosity, and even love toward him or her.[26]

However,

> New research suggests that harboring feelings of betrayal may be linked to high blood pressure—which can ultimately lead to stroke, kidney or heart failure, or even death. A study done at University of Tennessee showed that "high" forgivers

---

[23]R. D. Enright and J. North, *Exploring Forgiveness* (Madison: University of Wisconsin Press, 1998).21

[24]Enright, 29.

[25]Enright, 94.

[26]Enright and Human Development Study Group (1994), "Piaget on the moral development of forgiveness. Identity or Reciprocity?" *Human Development.* 37, 63-80.

—those who forgive easily—had both a lower resting blood pressure and smaller increases in blood pressure rate than "low" forgivers—bigger grudge-holders.[27]

Psychologists find it difficult to define forgiveness. They think it is something mysterious that cannot be fully grasped. Brakehielm writes, "Defining forgiveness is ambiguous ... there is no single concept of forgiveness."[28] Bonar opposes his view that "the need for forgiveness is explained within every major system of psychology."[29] From this understanding, the psychological definition appears to focus on forgiveness as an action or an attitude on the part of the forgiver. The works of Enright shows that forgiveness is obtained from psychotherapy and it is understood from a cognitive position:

Forgiveness is the overcoming of negative affect and judgment toward the offender by denying ourselves the right to such effect and judgment, but by endeavoring to view the offender with benevolence, compassion, and even love while recognizing that he or she has abandoned the right to them.[30]

Four elements of forgiveness can be derived from the above study:

1.   the person who forgives has suffered a deep hurt, so he or she develops resentment;

---

[27]Pirisi, A., (2000). "Forgive To Live," *Psychology Today* .33 (4), 26.

[28]C. R. Brakenhielm, *Forgiveness*, (Minneapolis: Fortress Press, 1986), 35.

[29]C. A. Bonar, "Personality Theories and Asking Forgiveness," *Journal of Psychology and Christianity*, 8(1), 45-51.

[30]R. D. Enright and the Educational Psychology Group (1990), "Must a Christian require repentance before forgiving?" *Journal of Psychology and Christianity*, 9 (3), 16-19; R. D. Enright, E. Gassin, and C. Wu, (1992), "Forgiveness: A Developmental View," *Journal of Moral Education*, 21 (2), 99-114; R. D. Enright and the Human Development Study Group (1991), "The Moral Development of Forgiveness" in W. Kurtines, & J. Gewirtz (ed.), *Handbooks of Moral Behavior and Development*, Hillsdale, N. J; Erlbaum, pages 123-152.

2. the offended person has a moral right to resentment but overcomes it nonetheless;

3. a new response to the offending party occurs showing compassion and love; and

4. this loving response occurs despite the realization that there is no obligation to love the offender.

Forgiveness involves the affective, cognitive and behavioural systems that are manifested in how a person forgives the offender and feels, thinks, and behaves towards him or her. According to psychological thinking, forgiveness is the absence of a negative effect, judgment and behaviour towards the perpetrator. However, forgiveness needs to integrate cognitive, effective behavioural and volitional, motivational, spiritual, religious and interpersonal approaches. Thus the spiritual dimension of forgiveness is an important component of forgiveness as well as the volitional element. Pingleton writes, "The spiritual dimension of forgiveness is an important component of forgiveness and volitional element."[31] It is true that the volitional dimension in forgiveness plays an important role, yet to the human, our faculties are mobilized in forgiving others based on compassion, heart, intellect, judgment, imagination, and faith. Indeed, forgiveness is more than a substitution of hateful feelings with loving feelings. For instance, a survivor of sexual abuse is likely to keep both the good and bad aspects of the perpetrator in view. If this happens, forgiveness will allow the survivor to absorb the full evil of the abuse that was committed against the person at the same time, not losing sight of the perpetrator. On the other hand, forgiveness in psychotherapy considers the cognitive

---

[31]J. P. Pingleton, *Why we Don't Forgive: Diagnosis and Treatment of Failures in the Forgiveness Process*, (Kansas: Christian Association for Psychological Studies, 1993), 23.

dimensions in emotive aspects of dealing with hurt and resentment thinking it would heal hurts. There are others in the field of psychology who understand forgiveness as a "wilful process in which the forgiver does not retaliate, rather he or she responds to the offender in a loving way." For example, Walter sees forgiveness as

> a voluntary process that usually requires courage; multiple acts of the will to complete. To forgive is to give up all claim on the offender including letting go of the emotional consequences of the hurt.[32] His view is interesting in the sense that the person who has been hurt has two alternatives—to be destroyed by resentment, which leads to death, or to forgive which leads to healing and life.

Therefore, psychological literature tends to focus on the benefits of forgiveness for the forgiver and the role of forgiveness in the therapeutic and healing process. According to their theories, forgiveness is spiritual or transpersonal as well as interpersonal and put it that forgiveness has qualities that transcend one's relationship with the person being forgiven and opens the forgiver to himself or herself and world in new ways. However, it is more than interpersonal quality. In this regard, psychologists speak of the experience of forgiveness in terms of its qualities of gift and grace, which is often described as a bridge between psychology and theology.

------

[32]R. P. Walters, *Forgiving: An Essential Element in Effective Living: Studies in Formative Spirituality*, 5(3), 365-374.

BIBLIOGRAPHY

Affinito, A. G. *When to Forgive: A Healing Guide to Help You Come to Terms with Your Emotions.* Oakland: New Harbinger, 1999.

Augsburger, David W. *Helping People Forgive.* Louisville: Westminster & John Knox Press, 1996.

__________. *Caring Enough to Forgive: True Forgiveness.* Ventura: Regal Books, 1981.

Bergan, Jacqueline Syrup. *Forgiveness: A Guide to Prayer.* Winona, Minnesota: Christian Brother's Publication, 1966.

Casarjian, R. *Forgiveness: A Bold Choice for a Peaceful Heart.* New York: Bantam Books, 1992.

Collins, Grey. *Christian Counselling: A Comprehensive Guide.* Third Edition. Dallas: Thomas Nelson, 2007.

Davis, L. *I Thought We Had Never Speak Again: The Road from Estrangement to Reconciliation.* New York: Harper Collins, 2002.

Delashmutt, Gary. *Loving God's Way.* USA: Xenos Publishing, 1966.

Ensor, John. *Experiencing God's Forgiveness.* Colorado Springs: NavPress, 1997.

Enright, R.D, & J. North. *Exploring Forgiveness.* Madison: University of Wisconsin, Press, 1998.

Flanigan, B. *Forgiving the Unforgivable: Overcoming the Bitter Legacy of Intimate Wounds.* New York: McMillian, 1992.

Ferguson, Sinclair B. (Ed). *New Dictionary of Theology.* Leicester: Intervarsity Press, 1998.

Inrig, Gary. *Forgiveness.* Grand Rapids, Michigan: Discovery House Publishers, 2005.

Leslie, Parrot. *When Bad Things Happen to Good Marriages.* Grand Rapids, Michigan: Zondervan Publishing House, 2001.

Lewis, Smedes. *Forgive And Forget: Healing The Hurts We Don't Deserve.* San Francisco. Harper and Row Publishers, 1984.

Luskin, F. *Forgive for God: A Proven Prescription for Health and Happiness.* New York: HarperSanfracisco, 2002.

McCullough, M.E., K.L Pargament, & C.E. Thoresen. *Forgiveness: Theory, Research, and Practice.* New York: Guilford Press, 2000.

Meyer, Paul J. *Forgiveness: The Ultimate Miracle.* USA: Thomas Nelson Publishers, 2006.

Myers, Glenn. *Cathy's Story: Learning To Forgive.* Great Britain: Christian Focus Publications, 1997.

Minnow, Martha. *Between Vengeance and Forgiveness.* Boston: Beacon Press, 1998.

Nelson, M.B. *The Unburdened Heart: 5 Keys to Forgiveness and Freedom.* New York: Harper, 2000.

Oliver, J. P. "Salach". *New International Dictionary of Old Testament Theology and Exegesis.* Grand Rapids, Michigan: Baker Academic, 2007.

Roger, J. *Forgiveness: The Key to the Kingdom.* Los Angeles: Mandeville, 1994.

Smedes, L.B. *Forgive and Forget: Healing the Hurts We Don't Deserve.* New York: Pocket Books, 1984.

Strauss, Robert. *The Power of Forgiving.* Kaduna: Evangel Publishing, 2000.

Stott, John. *The Contemporary Christian.* Leicester: InterVarsity Press, 1992.

Yancey, Philip. *What Is So Amazing About Grace?.* Grand Rapids, Michigan: Zondervan Publishing House, 2001.

www.ingramcontent.com/pod-product-compliance
Lightning Source LLC
Chambersburg PA
CBHW050526160726

48003CB00001B/476